M000209053

Before My Warranty Runs Out

Human, Transgender, and Environmental Rights Advocate

by

Joanna (Sister Mary Elizabeth) Clark

and

Margot Wilson

Transgender Publishing

an imprint of

Castle Carrington Publishing

Victoria, BC

Canada

2021

Before My Warranty Runs Out

Human, Transgender, and Environmental Rights Advocate

First published in paperback in 2021

Cover Photo: Joanna Clark
Cover Design: Margot Wilson
All photographs from the author's private collection (except where otherwise noted):

ISBN: 978-1-990096-19-8 (paperback)
ISBN: 978-1-990096-20-4 (Kindle electronic book)
ISBN: 978-1-990096-21-1 (Smashwords electronic book)

Published in Canada by
TransGender Publishing
www.transgenderpublishing.ca

an imprint of
Castle Carrington Publishing Group
www.castlecarringtonpublishing.ca
Victoria BC
Canada

Contents

Preface

A Story Most Deserving

Enlisting in the US Navy as a young man, rising to the rank of Chief Petty Officer, certified as a Master Professional Association of Divers Instructor (PADI) and saturation diver, transitioning in her mid-30s in 1974 before the word transgender was in common use,[1] recruited into the Army as a woman, successfully suing the Department of the Army for wrongful dismissal, speaking to college and university classes to increase the visibility of trans issues, advocating for changes in government identity documentation for trans people, making vows as an Episcopalian Sister, and founder of the world's largest online HIV/AIDS database, Joanna (Sister Mary Elizabeth) Clark has lived a life filled with adventure, near-death experiences, family, faith, and advocacy, a life story most deserving of the telling.

Joanna and I first met in the spring of 2017 through an introduction facilitated by our mutual friend Jude Patton. Agreeing to collaborate on writing her life story, we proceeded to meet by Skype on a more-or-less weekly basis as she shared the stories of her extraordinary life. We have managed to meet face-to-face several times and, in the end,

---

[1] See KJ Rawson's discussion of the origin of the word "transgender" https://www.thenewsminute.com/article/debunking-origin-behind-word-transgender. It is important to remark here that Joanna prefers the word "transsexual" to describe herself for, as she says, she has always been female: she has only changed her body to comply with her perception of her authentic self (see footnote 56).

we have amassed some 150 hours of recorded conversations. Now, 4 years later (almost to the day), Joanna's story, *Before My Warranty Runs Out: Human, Trans, and Environmental Advocate* is available.

Our Skype conversations were recorded and I had them transcribed.[2] Subsequently, I sent the transcriptions to Joanna and she used them as memory aids as she took the first pass at writing her story. As we sent the chapters back and forth electronically between us, we have revised, commented on, and edited the chapters into the form that follows. Joanna also contributed exerpts from this manuscript to *Glimmerings: Trans Elders Tell Their Stories* edited by Margot Wilson and Aaron Devor[3] and *TRANScestors, Volume II: Generations of Change* edited by Jude Patton and Margot Wilson.[4]

Joanna's stories create a vibrant tapestry of challenge, courage, joy, resolute determination, hope, humour, and love. Her straightforward, no nonsense storytelling style draws the reader in and holds them in thrall through to the end, which isn't really an ending, of course, but simply the beginning of a new chapter. At almost 83, Joanna remains a powerful and engaged advocate for human, trans, and environmental rights.

---

[2] The recorded conversations and transcriptions will be donated to the Transgender Archives at the University of Victoria libraries in Victoria, British Columbia, Canada, https://www.uvic.ca/transgenderarchives/.

[3] "The Question I Could Never Answer," TransGender Publishing, 2019, https://transgenderpublishing.ca/glimmerings-recognition-authenticity-and-gender-variance/.

[4] "I'm Still Here," TransGender Publishing, 2020, https://transgenderpublishing.ca/live-trips-vol-ii-generations-of-change/.

For me, it has been a great priviledge and pleasure to serve as audience, wordsmith, and collaborator in the telling of the story of Joanna's life to date.

Margot Wilson
March 2021

Editors note: Based on Joanna's experience being sight challenged—an issue she does not discuss in this version of her life story—we decided to publish this volume in 14 point font with lots of white space to support those who have seeing challenges. E-book versions of *Before My Warranty Runs Out* allow readers to further increase the size of the print for ease of reading.

Early Years

My father married the boss's daughter in Harvey, Illinois on 17 June 1934. His father-in-law's wedding gift was his termination to avoid the appearance of nepotism. So, the next morning my father and his new bride moved to Pontiac, Michigan. Four years later, on 16 June 1938, I arrived. Christened Michael Forbes Clark, I was their only child.

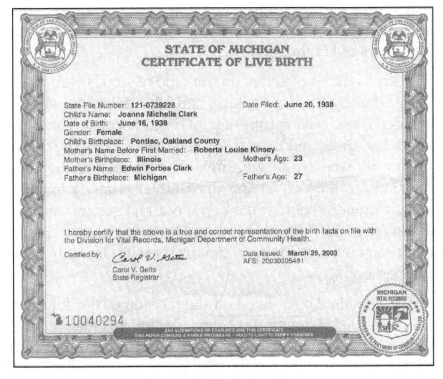

STATE OF MICHIGAN
CERTIFICATE OF LIVE BIRTH

State File Number: 121-0739228   Date Filed: June 20, 1938
Child's Name: Joanna Michelle Clark
Date of Birth: June 16, 1938
Gender: Female
Child's Birthplace: Pontiac, Oakland County
Mother's Name Before First Married: Roberta Louise Kinsey
Mother's Birthplace: Illinois   Mother's Age: 23
Father's Name: Edwin Forbes Clark
Father's Birthplace: Michigan   Father's Age: 27

I hereby certify that the above is a true and correct representation of the birth facts on file with the Division for Vital Records, Michigan Department of Community Health.

Certified by: *Carol V. Getts*   Date Issued: March 26, 2003
                                          AFS: 20030305481
Carol V. Getts
State Registrar

10040294

ANY ALTERATIONS OR ERASURES VOID THIS CERTIFICATE
THIS PAPER CONTAINS A VISIBLE WATERMARK – HOLD TO LIGHT TO VERIFY PRESENCE

Figure 1: Birth Certificate
Note: Change of name to Joanna Michelle on birth certificate

I hid my gender problems until I was in my 30s and thinking about what I could write about my life is difficult because my coming out wasn't until 1973. Actually, it was January of 1974 when I came out. By the time I was about three or four years old, I knew that I was somehow different, but I had no words to describe what or how I felt.

I don't remember much about my early years. From early pictures and stories told to me by my parents, my earliest playmates were young girls. All of my parent's closest friends had daughters, and almost all of my playmates were girls. However, I don't remember having any particular emotional feelings about it at the time.

It wasn't until we moved to a new house on Lewis Street that I met the first boys close to my age. I was about two and a half years old at the time.

There were five houses on our side of Lewis Street. The Johnson family lived next door, and Mrs. Johnson, with her daughter's aid, was raising her twin grandsons. The boys' mother had died, and their father died at Pearl Harbor. They were not allowed to play with any of the children on the street. Sometimes, if they sat on the edge of their property to talk to us, their grandmother would come out and scream at them, "Get in the house." She did not want them socializing. In fact, I can't remember them ever socializing with anybody in the neighborhood.

The Donahue boys lived on the far side of the Johnsons. Billie was four, Tommy three, and Danny was one year old. While we were friends, we seldom played together. I did play with the younger Donohue boy but by the late part of my third or fourth year, I was beginning to feel that I just didn't belong with the boys.

My closest friend was Sandra, who was my age. I lost her in the summer of 1943, shortly after our fifth birthdays, to leukemia. My mother told me I was devastated by her loss.

The remaining two families on the far end of the street had daughters, but they were four to five years older, and they seldom interacted with us.

Right behind us, the family had two daughters who were close to my age and I played with them sometimes. I preferred to play with the girls and throughout my grade school years, my primary playmates were the girls in my school classes. Weekends, my mother would often drop me off for the day at the home of one of my classmates. She lived out at one of the lakes and I would spend Saturdays and most Sundays over there with her and her friends.

At that time, I don't know if it was so much feelings of being a girl: it was more like comfort. I enjoyed playing house with the girls, taking care of the babies, and playing with the dolls rather than playing with boys. With the boys, I just never fit in. I did not like the rough and tough stuff and I didn't play ball. Not that I didn't try. It just wasn't me and to the best of my ability, I avoided sports in school altogether. In grade school, the classroom was somewhat divided, with the girls on one side, the boys on the other. I wasn't allowed to sit on the girl's side. I tried but the best I could do was to sit on the aisle across from the girls.

On the opposite side of Lewis Street was the home of Saint Michael's Catholic School, Church, Clergy House, Convent, Community Center, and playground. The Convent was directly across the street from our front porch, and I would often invite myself over to sit on the porch with the sisters and talk with them about life as a sister.

Prior to the move to Lewis Street, my only playmates had been girls. But once we moved to Lewis Street, the conflict began. I was expected to be a boy and play with the boys. It all seemed so foreign to me. Unable to understand my feelings, nowhere to turn for information, and afraid to discuss my feelings with my parents, I would hide my feelings the best I could into my mid-30s.

I was maybe seven years old when I really started feeling that something was wrong. It was distressing only because I could not put my finger on it exactly. Sometimes, I questioned why I always felt more comfortable with the girls than I did with the boys. For example, in gym when we had to go into the locker room to take a shower, I just would not do it. I would not take a shower with the boys. I would hide in a corner and change my clothes and get out of there as quickly as possible.

Sometimes, the teacher would say, "You didn't take a shower."

I would answer, "No, but I'm going to be late." And I'd run off.

But at that time, I can't remember actually thinking or saying that I was supposed to be a girl. Certainly, I favored girls' things. I was more at home with girls' things to wear, but, of course, I wasn't allowed to wear them.

I remember when I was eight years old, I told my parents I was going to be a nun when I grew up. My family wasn't Catholic, but I went to the Catholic church because it was right across the street from our house. Actually, the convent for the nuns was right across the street and the church was a little bit off to the side.

Anyway, there were only two Protestant families in a two-block area, my family, and the neighbors next door. So, I ended up going with the Donohue family to the Catholic church. Of course, in those days, it was before Vatican II, so everything was in Latin. One day after mass, I told my parents that I was going to become a Catholic sister when I grew up. The next thing I knew I was going to the Baptist church.

༄

The United States entered the Second World War on 7 December 1941, following the Japanese attack on Pearl Harbor. My uncle dropped out of college and joined the US Army Air Corps. There was a shortage of pilots, so my uncle became one of the first "Flying Sergeants."

My father applied for the draft, but he had the skills needed to support the war effort. Throughout the war, he worked a double shift, building heavy trucks, tanks, and planes. I have few memories of him until after the war ended. By then, I was seven years old.

The war ended on 2 September 1945, and Mom and Dad decided to move to California to join Dad's brothers. They rented out our house, and in late-November 1945, we headed west. We stopped in Aurora, Illinois, to visit briefly with my mother's parents and then headed for route 66 and southern California.

We stayed in Glendale with Ken, Dad's older brother, for about three months. Dad could not find a full-time job, so we moved up to Santa Maria, where my uncle Kelly (the "Flying Sergeant") lived with his wife and children. After three more months of trying to find a permanent job, Dad decided it was time to head home to Pontiac, where he knew he had a good job with General Motors.

My Uncle, the "Flying Sergeant"

I mentioned that my Uncle Kelly was a subtle influence on me. Actually, I idolized him and his miliary career, which began in 1941, just before he turned 20. He dropped out of college and entered the first class of flying sergeants as a "Buck Private" and trained to fly the new Lockheed P38 Lightening aircraft (see https://tinyurl.com/bklgm4h). Assigned to a squadron operating out of North Africa, the "flying sergeant" became known as one of the earliest US aces of World War II.

In 1943, my uncle was shooting down a German bomber (his eighth kill) when his new, inexperienced wingman maneuvered behind him and, in his excitement, triggered his 20-millimeter cannon and shot him down.

Unaware as to who had shot him, Uncle Kelly could only roll his plane over, push himself out, and pop his parachute. He was at about four hundered feet when his chute opened. He swung down once, but, on the second swing, he landed in three feet of water near Tunis, Algeria, blinded from swollen eyes and temporarily paralyzed below the waist. He was captured by residents who turned him over to the Italian military. They took him to the hospital, treated his wounds, and then, took him to an Italian prison. A month or two later, they announced that the Germans were going to take control of the prisoners and move them to Germany. So, he escaped and spent a hundred days behind enemy lines before he made it to the British lines. He received a Second Lieutenant commission and the Distinguished Flying Cross, and stayed in the Air Force for 25 years, flying B47 bombers (see https://tinyurl.com/y6v9g55l). Of course, the family always looked up to him and expected me to be the same. So, I hid my feelings and gender confusion until the early 1970s.

I returned to school at Baldwin Elementary to find that I was a full grade ahead of my classmates. But, instead of moving me forward to the third grade, I had to repeat the second grade.

In the third grade, I made friends with two girls, and we became inseparable. I would spend virtually every Saturday playing house with them. They treated me more like a girlfriend than a boyfriend. If only I could have told them. Finally, we graduated from elementary school and moved on to Junior High School. Unfortunately, we lived in different school districts, so I didn't see them daily until senior high school. Our Saturday get-togethers gradually ended after a couple of months.

࿐

When I was a teenager, the things I was involved in were not the usual things teenage boys are interested in. As I've said, I didn't participate in sports programs. I did try basketball one semester, but I didn't stay with it. I went for maybe six weeks in junior high, then made an excuse. It just wasn't for me.

I did get involved in the band for a while. I wanted to play the clarinet or the flute. But I was a monotone[5] and the instructor said, "Monotones make better drummers." So, I ended up being a drummer. I was not happy about that although it wasn't so bad after I learned to play the xylophone.

---

[5] A sound or voice that stays on the same note, https://dictionary.cambridge.org/us/dictionary/english/monotone.

Except one night, when we were giving a concert, I lost my place and when it came to the end, I went da-da-doo-da-da-dee-da. I kept going. After that, I wasn't allowed to play the xylophone anymore.

I thought I would be in the band when I got to high school. Pontiac had the number one marching band in the country, but the teacher expected us to fall in at five o'clock every morning and practice music for three hours before school started. Learning that, I decided that I didn't want to participate in band anymore. I wasn't that interested in school either. So, in a class of 492 students, I graduated 491st. My one interest at the time was amateur radio.

It wasn't until Christine Jorgensen hit the front page of Parade Magazine in 1952 that I finally pieced it together. I was 13 at that time and when I read Christine's story, it was the first time that I realized I was not alone. There were other people like me. Still, I never made contact with anybody until I got into the gender program at Stanford. Christine was the first exposure anybody in our area had to the idea that being transsexual was possible. Still, I kept my feelings secret because I had already learned how people referred to gays and I knew that I did not want to acknowledge what my feelings were.

Curiously, sometime after I started my transition, my dad asked me one day, "I keep hearing this term 'queer as a three-dollar bill.' What does that mean?"

I said, "You are talking about homosexuals."

He responded, "Homosexuals, what is that?"

I mean, here's a person who was in his late 60s or early 70s when he asked that question. The only term he was familiar with was "fag." He knew it applied to some males, but he didn't seem to know why. That has always amazed me.

But then, we grew up at a time when sex was a subject you really didn't bring up. In those days, discussion of any sexual behavior was taboo. This was before the women's rights movement and when women started getting "uppity" and striving to take back their rights, the push back was horrible. In those years, we were expected to be barefoot and pregnant, or perhaps a schoolteacher or maybe a nurse.

From that point on, I wanted to tell my parents but their negative reaction to Christine's story caused me to draw into myself even further. I thought, *I am an only child, what happens when they find out?* I was afraid, so I just hid my feelings as best I could. I put the article under my mattress, but my mother found it and tossed it into the trash. All I was thinking was, *How do I get it back?* It was not like today when you can go on the Internet and find it.

For me, reading Christine's story was like a lightbulb going on from the standpoint that all of a sudden, I realized, "Hey, I am not alone." It was like having the windows opened, an "OMG"[6] moment. All of a sudden there it was, the question that I could never answer. I had always known there was something there, but I just didn't know what it was. I knew that I was more comfortable around young girls—not to date them or anything like that—I just liked their company. I felt comfortable playing with dolls, but I simply couldn't ever put my finger on it—to think that I was in the wrong body, in the wrong gender. It wasn't until Christine that I

---

[6] Oh my God (also Oh my Goodness or Oh my Gosh), a common abbreviation, often used in SMS messages and Internet communication, used to express surprise, excitement, disbelief, https://en.wikipedia.org/wiki/OMG, https://en.oxforddictionaries.com/definition/omg.

finally had that "ah ha!" moment. That is what is wrong. That is what has been wrong all along. I think at that point I realized that this was the answer: I was in the wrong body. Maybe that was why I never wanted to be seen naked. For me, the idea of changing sex never came to mind until I read Christine's story, and I finally understood what was wrong. Then, all I could think about was, *How do I resolve the problem without losing my family?*

As a teenager, I was a ham radio operator. It was the only thing I had an interest in, at least until I learned about SCUBA[7] diving. My love for SCUBA diving began with the release of the movie *Creature from the Black Lagoon.* The evening I went to see the film, the Michigan Muck Combers, a local SCUBA club, was in the lobby, and I signed up for a lesson. My first dive was in four feet of water and lasted less than 10 minutes, and like flying, I was hooked.

I was 13 when I started diving. In those days, the sport was in its infancy. So, I had to dive by myself because there was nobody else to dive with. When I started diving, there were only six or seven adults in the whole state who were diving. Tom Mook started the Michigan Muck Combers and he taught me how to dive. I saved my money and got myself a tank and regulator. You could say I was hooked. I liked diving because I could be free. I could be myself down there. And I liked the ham radio for the same reason. I could be myself and no one would ever know who I really was. I was just a name on the radio.

Similarly, my fascination with flying began when I was 11 or 12. My dad had a friend who owned a Piper Cub, and

---

[7] Acronym for Self-Contained Underwater Breathing Apparatus.

he took me up a couple of times. By the second flight, I was hooked.

My dad thought that I should go into the military and be like my uncle the "Flying Sergeant." I had screwed up in school and didn't get my college degree before I joined the Navy. If I had, I could have been a commissioned officer, and I could have gone to flight school.

US Navy Reserve Years—(1955-1957)

A military career should have been the last thing on my mind, given my struggle with my gender identity. So, why did I join? There were five things in my life that I attribute to my joining the military.

I loved flying,

I loved SCUBA diving,

I loved electronics, and I had held an amateur radio license (W8ODE) since I was 13,

Subtle pressure to be like my Uncle Kelly, a "Flying Sergeant" who became one of the earliest US flying aces of World War II, who escaped a prisoner-of-war camp by walking 100 miles through Italy across German lines, and

An active military draft.

I thought, *Well, I really like SCUBA diving and there was the Underwater Demolition Team (UDT), and they were using SCUBA equipment. I'll go into the UDT and Mom and Dad will be proud of me. They will never have to know about how I really feel.*

When I told them that I wanted to go into the UDT, they just laughed at me.

They said "Are you out of your mind? You wouldn't make it through the door!"

And that was true. The guys who were working in the UDT were big and muscular. I was just a scrawny kid. I had muscles, but they were not developed to any great extent.

Also, I had virtually no body hair and barely any facial hair, which, actually, I was quite happy about.

≈

The Navy offered opportunities to both fly and SCUBA dive. They also offered what they called the "6N2 program." The six-year program included one year of reserve service during the last year of high school, followed by two years of active duty, and ended with three years of reserve service, thus avoiding the draft. Another factor that helped was my electronics background and my amateur radio license, which allowed me to enlist as an E3 instead of an E1 recruit.

So, four months into my 17th year, I talked my parents into granting permission for me to enlist in the US Naval Reserve. On 12 October 1955, I was sworn in as an E3 Seaman, attached to Naval Reserve Surface Division 9-104. In February 1956, I transferred to Air Wing Staff 71 at Naval Air Station (NAS) Grosse Ile, Michigan. My classification changed from Seaman to Airman.

During the Easter school vacation period (25 March to 7 April 1956), I went to boot camp at the Great Lakes Naval Training Center. The first morning there, they made battalion assignments–i.e., Acting Chief Petty Officer, etc. I was the only E3: the remainder were E1 (recruit) rank.

The Chief Petty Officer in charge of our battalion assigned the Acting Chief Petty Officer position to an E1. I drew the first watch, and the Chief walked me over to where I would be standing watch.

I don't remember what the Chief said precisely, but I remember responding, "I don't understand. They are all E1 recruits."

He replied, "So?"

I told him, "I'm not an E1. I'm an E3 Airmen."

The Chief had just picked names at random off the roster. Had he looked before he made his selections, he would have noticed that I had three stripes, not one. Now, he had a problem. As they say in the military, "Rank has its privileges."

We returned to the barracks, and he announced that I was the Acting Chief Petty Officer because of my current rank. The individual initially appointed Acting Chief Petty Officer now had my watch duties, and he was not happy. I learned quite a bit about Navy life and what was expected of us during my two weeks at Great Lakes. An hour after graduation from boot camp, I was on the train heading home. It was back to high school with a year till graduation.

US Navy Active Duty—School Years (1957-1958)

I graduated from high school on 26 June 1957. The next morning, I was on a Greyhound bus bound for the Naval Receiving Station, Philadelphia, Pennsylvania. I spent about six weeks at the Receiving Station being processed.

During my second week at the Receiving Station, my parents forwarded my draft notice to me. I wrote the Draft Board and told them, "Sorry, you are too late." I had joined the Navy.

Still, life in the Navy was difficult for me because we lived in a barracks[8] and took communal showers. I requested Aviation Electronics School but was declared ineligible. I would have to extend my enlistment by a year in order to go to aviation electronics school. I asked, "Where do I sign?" and became a so-called Airdale[9]—the term the Navy used to define aviation personnel. Little did I know that would lead me into service in the Vietnam war.

---

[8] A barrack is a building where military personnel live, usually used in the plural as barracks, comes from the Spanish word *barraca* for "soldier's tent," https://www.vocabulary.com/dictionary/barrack.

[9] Naval aviators, also known as "brown shoe aviators," a reference to the brown oxfords worn only by naval aviators (regular naval officers wore black shoes), any enlisted person onboard a Navy carrier whose job is directly associated with aircraft, http://www.cannon-lexington.com/Other%20Stories/Airedales.html, https://www.urbandictionary.com/define.php?term=Airdale.

I received orders for the nine-week Aviation Familiarization course at the Naval Air Technical Training Center (NATTC) in Norman, Oklahoma, to be followed by a 21-week course in Aviation Electronics at NATTC Memphis, Tennessee. The course would be expanded by an additional nine weeks before graduation to accommodate increasing system specialization. Graduating Aviation Electronics Technician (AT), students would now be designated ATN (Navigation), ATR (Radar), or ATS (Anti-Submarine Warfare). I requested the ATS syllabus, which would limit my assignments to land-based Patrol Squadrons, carrier-based anti-submarine squadrons, Naval Air Stations, or aircraft carriers.

It was there that I ran into my first wall. The Division Officer wanted me to drop out right then and there.

He said, "You will never make it through aviation electronics school. You will fail."

I told him I would graduate first in my class, and I did, thanks in part to my interest in amateur radio and the experience I had gained over the years. But while everybody else was going on liberty every night, I didn't participate. Although I was invited to join the group, I was pretty much a loner. Each night, I spent my free time at the library. While everyone else was heading off-base to the bars or a movie, I would return to the barracks after the library closing time, hit the rack, and get some sleep. My social life was virtually zero.

&

My time in Norman, Oklahoma, was fascinating. There, I had my first real experience with racism. People of color had separate toilets, drinking fountains, and all that stuff: plus, they not only had to ride at the back of the bus, but they also had to give up their seat to a white person if no seats were available.

I met my great aunt, Susanna Madora Salter,[10] for the second time, in Norman. I was six or seven years old the first time we met, and I have no memories of that first meeting except that she lived at the top of a high hill in Topeka, Kansas.

I was traveling with my parents on our way to California in 1945. Now, it was 1957, and she was in a Board and Care home. Once I arrived, I introduced myself, and every Saturday, if I had the day off, I would go to visit with her. She was fabulous to talk to because, in 1887, she became the first woman to be elected to public office in the United States, and, oh boy, did she have stories to tell. She lived to be 101 plus two weeks. She was amazing.

ॐ

While most students spent their liberty chasing women at the local bars, I spent my liberty with my nose in the books. While I had screwed up in high school, I was giving up an additional year of my life to attend these schools. I was not about to screw up this opportunity. School had a nice additional benefit. In addition to getting an education, the person graduating with the highest grade received their first choice of duty station. I intended to go to a Patrol Squadron based in either Bermuda or Hawaii to fly and dive, so I had to do well in school.

---

[10] Learn more about Aunt Susanna see https://www.kshs.org/p/kansas-historical-quarterly-susanna-madora-salter/13106.

As promised, I graduated first in my class and I was able to choose my first duty station. Because of my love for SCUBA diving, I selected Patrol Squadron 49, located at the Naval Operating Base (NOB) in Bermuda. My weekends were spent snorkeling and eventually SCUBA diving when the first dive shop opened in Hamilton.

Patrol Squadron FORTY-NINE (1958-1961)

I graduated in May 1958 and received orders to Patrol Squadron FORTY-NINE (VP-49), Naval Operating Base (NOB), Bermuda.

VP-49 would be my home for the next 34 months. My rank on arrival was E3, ATSAN. Five months later, in September 1958, I advanced to E4, Aviation Electronics Technician ASW Specialist Petty Officer 3rd Class (Designated ATS3).

VP-49's aircraft consisted of P5M-1 and P5M-2 Martin Marlins.

Figure 2: P5M-1 assigned to VP-49 in flight near NOB Bermuda
with what appears to be a feathered starboard engine
Note: LP squadron designation on the tail
Photo credit: US Navy National Museum of Naval Aviation

My arrival at VP-49 was rather strange, as my rank was E3 (ATSAN), but I was treated more like an E4 (ATS3) Petty Officer. Upon arrival, the norm for an E2 (Airmen Apprentice) or E3 (Airmen) was an assignment to the galley or barracks for janitorial services for six months. Petty Officers (E4 and above) would go directly to a shop or an aircrew. I went straight to the electronics shop, where I worked for the next four months as the shop's electronic parts supply clerk. I could not help but question these events in my mind.

"Why was I being treated differently?"

Figure 3: P5M-2 assigned to VP-49 taking off from Great Sound, near NOB Bermuda
Note: LP squadron designation on the tail
Photo credit: US Navy National Museum of Naval Aviation

Also, because I never went to bars or chased women, and my physical appearance—no body hair and not very muscular—raised questions about my sexuality. More than once, I had to endure, "He's probably queer," or "Are you queer?"

To their question, I always replied, "No, I'm not. I just have other priorities. While you are going out and having a good time, I go to the library and have a good time reading and expanding my knowledge so I can make rank."

In the end, I made rank, and they didn't.

After this "getting acquainted" period, I moved to the AN/ASQ-8 Magnetic Anomaly Detection (MAD) maintenance shop. During this period, the hazing began over the question of, "How, or why, did I avoid galley or barracks duty when I first arrived."

I finally got my answer—at least I thought I had the answer. In May 1959, the Commanding Officer announced that we (VP-49) were receiving the Fleet Air Wing 5 (FAW-5) Operational Readiness award. Admiral Clark, the Commanding Officer of FAW-5, would be presenting the award.

During the award ceremony, for whatever reason (I will never know), the Admiral walked past me in formation, stopped, turned, and walked back to me, where he turned to faced me, and asked, "How do you like the squadron, son?"

I said, "Fine, Sir."

He replied, "Nice to hear that."

With that, he finished his inspection without speaking to another soul.

Now, the rumors were no longer rumors. I had the answer to the question that had bugged me since my arrival. Someone on the officer staff had somehow gotten the idea that I was the Admiral's son, and in time, the rumor had spread to the enlisted men. No matter how strong my denial was, I was the Admiral's son in the eyes of my shipmates.

In June 1959, I was sent back to NAS Norfolk for more schooling, this time to the AN/APS-44 radar and radio operator schools. I was supposed to be back in Bermuda by mid-July, but a freak water-skiing accident put me in the hospital when a broken board on the ski jump came loose and ripped a previous surgery site open.[11]

My original plan had been to complete school, return to Bermuda for four weeks, then take leave to fly home to Pontiac and get married, partially to put an end to the suggestion that I was gay. The accusations had begun early on in my naval career and it seemed to me that the only solution was to get married. As it turned out, I finished the last week of school after being released from Portsmouth Naval Hospital. Then, I flew directly to Pontiac for the wedding.

ॐ

I had met my wife in high school. She was in 10th grade when I was a senior. She worked in the truant office as part of her job experience to be a secretary. I was skipping school an awful lot at that time. Actually, I had quit school to join the Navy, but I was turned down because I had a hernia and a varicocele.[12] So, I had to have that taken care of first. After I had the surgery, my dad made it very clear.

---

[11] A hernia and a varicocele repair.

[12] A varicose vein in the scrotum, https://mnurology.com/condition-varicoceles.php.

"If you want a home, you will have to go back to school. Otherwise, there is the door."

So, I ended up going back to high school again.

I was a regular processing through the truant office and that is how I met her. She decided to latch onto me, engaging me in conversation and, eventually, we began dating. I took her to the prom. Truthfully, if I hadn't had a relationship with her, I would not have gone to the prom. I had no desire to go.

I left for the Navy the day after graduation and she corresponded with me. Then, when the "You're not gay, are you?" picked up in Bermuda, I gave in to marriage. I was being pretty selfish because I knew that my transsexualism would eventually come out. My mind was in overdrive thinking about what could happen then. Not only would I be ruining her life, I would be kicked out of the service with a dishonorable discharge. I wouldn't have been able to live with that. My parents would have been very upset.

On 22 August 1959, I married Betsy Jane Wilkins (BJ).[13] The day after our wedding, on the morning of 23 August, we flew to Bermuda, our home for the next two years, arriving at the Bermuda airport, St. George's Parish. From there, we took a taxi to Hogg Bay Flat, Somerset Parish, where I had made arrangements for us to stay at a bed and breakfast place.

I took BJ to the house and got her settled. Then, I left to check-in at the base. But when I got there, I got a great welcome when I walked into the squadron duty office.

---

[13] A pseudonym.

"Welcome back, Clark. There is some flight gear for you (helmet, flight suit, knife, and boots). You're flying on LP-11 to NAS Norfolk."

I asked, "When?"

"Right now!" the Lieutenant replied. "A hurricane is about to hit the island, and the squadron is evacuating all of the aircraft to Norfolk. We're short a radioman. So, you're going."

I called BJ at the B&B and gave her the bad news.

I said, "I will be back in two days. I have to go to Norfolk."

She asked, "Why?"

I said, "Because the hurricane is going to hit the island in about two hours. Seaplanes cannot withstand a hurricane. Because I am a qualified radio operator and they are short of qualified personnel, I have to fly."

Of course, it freaked her out. After all, she was young, and this was her first time away from home. She was in a foreign country. The only person she knew was abandoning her to escape a hurricane. She had every right to freak out.

In the end, I didn't make it to Norfolk. I went down to the fight-line, boarded the aircraft, and waited for the launch. An hour later, we were at 10,000 feet, 125 miles west of Bermuda, when—*bang!*—we lost our port engine. We turned around and limped back to Bermuda on our starboard engine. We made it in just before the storm hit.

After tying down the aircraft, I hitched a ride to the main gate and rode my bike back to the bed and breakfast. I knocked on the door and said, "I'm home." Saying that BJ was "freaked out" was an understatement.

She came to the door and said, "I thought you were going to Norfolk."

I said, "No, we decided to crash instead."

She didn't even ask, "Are you ok?" She just tore into me. But, a week later, she had settled down, and we found a new home at Foley's Cottage, Hogg Bay Flat, Somerset, Bermuda. I would say that was pretty much the beginning of the failure of our marriage. We stayed married for eleven years after she became pregnant. I stayed with her until she finally said, "I have had enough," and left. But, more about this later.

The rest of my tour with VP-49 was pretty standard. I flew as a radioman on LP-2, then transferred to LP-11 as First Technician. Off-duty time in Bermuda was terrific, at least in my book.

そ

The culture was much different than what either of us had experienced growing up in the United States. Most surprising was that, in Bermuda, there was no racial disparity based on skin color. Blacks and whites fell in love and routinely married—a refreshing change from the racism I had experienced in Norman and Memphis.

The most unsettling experience we had was the degree of hatred the Bermudians expressed towards Portuguese immigrants.

The first Portuguese arrived in Hamilton on 6 November 1849. In the years that followed, thousands of Portuguese immigrated to Bermuda to carve out a better life for themselves. But they found themselves relegated to second-class citizens' status, which was sadly still the norm during the years BJ and I lived on the island.

Unaware of the hatred towards the Portuguese when I first arrived, I had joined the Portuguese Baptist Church in Paget Parish. My membership in the Portuguese Baptist Church raised a few eyebrows on base whenever I mentioned which church I had joined.

BJ had the unique ability to adapt to the Bermudian dialect. She could pass very convincingly as a native-born Bermudian. She often used her ability to gain an advantage when dealing with the locals.

In December 1959, I developed complications from my surgery at Portsmouth Naval Hospital. The medical staff referred me to Kindley Air Force Base (AFB) hospital for evaluation. I underwent surgery, and after a week of in-hospital recovery, I was released home to VP-49 for two weeks of "no-duty" recovery.

The doctors at our Navy dispensary declared me fit for duty, however. I was in no condition to return to duty, so I put in for two weeks of sick leave. My division officer denied my request. I asked to see the Captain. He asked to see the surgery site, so I reluctantly dropped my drawers. He took one look at the six-inch incision that still had the stitches in place, let out a "Jesus Christ," and remarked, "What are you doing here? You should be in bed."

I told him that Kindley had released me for two weeks of bed rest and to have the Navy doctors remove the stitches this coming Monday. When I checked into the dispensary, however, the doctor returned me to full duty.

The Captain asked if my wife was looking after me, and I said, "Yes, Sir." He said he would see me in two weeks and let him know if I had any more problems with the Navy doctors at the dispensary. The following Monday, they removed the stitches, and I was welcomed back to work at the end of the second week.

῾

In March 1960, BJ greeted me with a big smile and informed me that she was pregnant.

Neither of us trusted the doctors at the naval dispensary, so we sought a local physician to be BJ's doctor. As a result, our son was born on 25 October 1960 at King Edward VII Memorial Hospital in Hamilton, with dual (US and Bermudian) citizenship.

I was not a good parent. I had to work two jobs to make ends meet financially. At that time, an Airman's salary was $99 a month. Of course, this was in 1958. When I made Third Class Petty Officer, my base pay was raised to $134 per month and when I got married, I got an additional $75 dependent allowance and $33 Comrats (for not eating in the commissary).[14] Not much to live on, especially if you live off-base. So, I worked two jobs and I was never home with my son when he was growing up. I was a Chief Petty Officer when I left the Navy in 1969.

In a way, it was so my son could have a good life that I worked so much, and I was totally occupied either teaching

---

[14] Commuted Rations, also basic allowance for subsistence (BAS), defined as a cash allowance payable to enlisted personnel who are permitted to mess separately in lieu of rations-in-kind when messing facilities are available, see
http://navyadministration.tpub.com/14163/css/Commuted-Rations-Basic-Allowance-For-Subsistence-61.htm.

school or working at my second job managing the amateur radio station on the base as a part of Special Services. There were quite a few nights that I came home and found the doors locked and blocked so that I couldn't get in.

To a large extent, working all the time kept me from thinking too much about my gender situation. More than anything, I believe working hard was a crutch to keep me from thinking. As long as I could keep myself occupied, I was fine—up to a point—but then it got harder and harder as time went on.

The remainder of my tour with VP-49 was pretty routine. I decided that I wanted to go to NATTC Memphis to teach electronics, but that meant I had to make Second Class Petty Officer before the end of April 1961. I would also need to reenlist.

NATTC Memphis, Tennessee (1961-1966)

In May 1961, I advanced to E5, Aviation Electronics Technician ASW Specialist Petty Officer 2nd Class (Designated ATS2), and I reenlisted for six-years. I received orders transferring me to NATTC Memphis, Tennessee, for a three-year instructor tour teaching electronics and ASW detection systems at the basic electronics (AT/A) school.

We arrived in Millington, Tennessee, in early June 1961, and I was assigned to Instructor School for three weeks of intense "how to be an instructor" training. Then, I was assigned to a branch of the AT/A school to complete the final two weeks of instructor training.

Tennessee had changed little since my last tour in 1958: racism was still rampant. The "N" word, used to describe a person of color, was seldom used openly in the Navy. Still, it was the only term used in the civilian population.

One of my colored friends, Ernie, whom I crewed with during our VP-49 tour, received orders to NATTC Memphis shortly after I was assigned there. Ernie had married a Bermudian girl, who, from all appearances, was white. Her father was black, so categorically, she was considered to be black as well. Their first child was born shortly before he received orders to NATTC Memphis.

The civil rights movement was still in its infancy. Rosa Parks[15,16] had set the movement in motion in December 1955. Still, the southern Whites were not going to extend equality to people of color without a fight.[17] Ernie, his wife, and his child's lives would be at risk throughout their tour of duty at NATTC Memphis.

I should also mention that their marriage was often perceived as interracial, which further complicated their situation. Interracial marriage did not become legal in the United States until 1967, Loving vs. Virginia. [18] Consequently, Ernie's wife carried her birth certificate, which included her racial designation, with her ID.

BJ and I, not realizing the depth of hatred that still existed towards people of color, had invited them to stay with us while getting checked into the base and being assigned base housing. Ernie and his family's arrival at our home in Millington elicited a negative response from our southern civilian neighbors when they saw an apparently white woman with a baby clinging to a person of color's arm. We had lunch, then headed out to the base to check them in.

The duty officer (DO) freaked out when he learned that the "white" woman with Ernie was his wife.

His initial response was, "What stupid SOB gave you orders here with a white wife? You realize this is the Deep South. If they see you together in town, they will hang you."

---

[15] https://en.wikipedia.org/wiki/Rosa_Parks.

[16] https://en.wikipedia.org/wiki/Montgomery_bus_boycott.

[17] https://en.wikipedia.org/wiki/Jim_Crow_laws.

[18] https://en.m.wikipedia.org/wiki/Interracial_marriage_in_the_United_States.

He continued, "We don't have any enlisted housing available right now. Where are you staying?"

I told the DO they would be staying with us.

He asked, "Where do you live?"

I told him, "In Millington."

The DO said, "The hell if you are. They will burn your house down with you in it, or they will hang you."

The DO got on the phone, and after a couple of calls, turned to us and told Ernie to "grab his things." The family would be staying in the visiting Admiral's quarters for the next week or two.

The DO, then, made it as clear as possible.

"You two will never go off base together unless friends from the base accompany you."

Ernie completed his three-year tour and returned to the fleet. Sadly, we lost contact with them over the next couple of years.

∾

As Christmas 1961 approached, BJ and I decided to take the first period of leave. The holiday leave periods were first come, first served, and broken into early (Christmas) and late (New Year) segments. I knew BJ would appreciate having the extra time to visit with her parents. They would enjoy the additional time to spoil their grandson.

I returned to duty on 27 December to find a letter asking me to attend my school's Alumni Association meeting in Washington, DC on 3 January 1962. I was a correspondence student at the Capitol Radio Engineering Institute (CREI)[19]. I had been elected 3rd Vice President of the Alumni Association.

I called my contact at CREI and told him that I had just returned from early leave, and to take leave now would be impossible. He asked me to try. So, I submitted my request as soon as I got to the office. The request was denied, as I had anticipated. I called my contact and told him I was sorry that I would be unable to come to the meeting.

He said, "Okay. I'll handle it."

I should have asked how.

An hour later, my Division Officer called me out of class and said, "The Commanding Officer (CO) wants to see you immediately."

I asked, "About what?"

He replied, "The special request that I denied."

So, I headed down to South 1 to see the CO.

I had no idea what the CO wanted. He invited me into his office, and I came to attention, saluted, and said, "Reporting as ordered, Sir."

He returned my salute and started in. It was clear; he was not happy. He asked, "Your division officer denied your leave request?"

I responded, "Yes, Sir."

"You were unhappy it was turned down?" he asked.

"No, Sir. I told them it would be turned down."

---

[19] https://en.wikipedia.org/wiki/Capitol_Technology_University.

He asked, "Then, why did you bother putting in for leave?"

"I did not want to be lying when I called them back to tell them it had been turned down."

The CO sat down. He looked at me for a moment, then asked, "Did you call anyone else?"

I said, "No one, Sir."

"Then, why would the Chief of Naval Operations (CNO) call me personally and ask me to approve your leave?"

I stood there, stunned for the moment. Then, I let out with an "Oh My God! That's what he meant."

The CO responded, "Who meant what?"

"My contact at CREI, Captain, is the CEO's Chief of Staff. He is the liaison between the Alumni Association and CREI Corporate."

"You're telling me," the Captain said, "that someone at CREI corporate has influence with the CNO?"[20]

"Yes, Sir. I believe so," I replied. "If you recall, Admiral Arleigh Burke[21] retired about six months ago."

"Yes. So what?"

"Well, Sir, Admiral Burke is the CEO of CREI, and the meeting I have been asked to attend is the annual meeting of the CREI Alumni Association. We are scheduled to meet at the White House with President Kennedy's Science Advisor,

---

[20] CNO is Chief of Naval Operations.

[21] https://en.wikipedia.org/wiki/Arleigh_Burke.

Jerome Wiesner, for lunch. My best guess is that my contact asked Admiral Burke to intercede."

My Division Officer greeted me upon my return to the office.

"Well?" he asked.

"The CO granted my leave," I said. "The CO even offered a staff car to take me to the airport, but I declined. My plane leaves at five pm."

The Division Chief joined the conversation, then, asking, "Who the hell are you visiting? The President?"

As I headed for the door, I replied over my shoulder, "Yes, I'm having lunch at the White House!"

ॐ

In May 1963, I advanced to E6, Aviation Electronics Technician ASW Specialist Petty Officer 1st Class. My three-year tour became a five-year tour, with an additional two years assigned to the advanced electronics (AT-B) school.

In the second year of my tour teaching in the AT/B school, I was assigned to teach a two-week introductory course in calculus. I told my Division Chief that I was not qualified, as I had only had one year of algebra in high school.

He said, "That's okay. You will sit through the course first."

I ended up sitting through it three times. I finally had no choice. I had to try. The first hour, in my opinion, did not go well. One of the students agreed and took me aside. He was a reservist E3 (Airman) on six months of active duty, and he had asked to go through the program. He offered to teach the course. I asked him what his qualifications were.

He said, "I am an Associate Professor of Mathematics at the University of California, Berkeley.

I handed him my chalk and told the class, "You have a new instructor."

It wasn't long before my Leading Chief looked in the door window and saw a student teaching the class. He opened the door and signaled me to join him in the hallway.

He, in not the friendliest voice, asked, "What the hell are you doing?"

I told him, "Learning calculus. He's great. I'm beginning to understand calculus for the first time."

My Chief asked who he was, and I told him, "He's an Associate Professor of Mathematics at UC Berkeley."

We re-entered the classroom together, and my Chief took a seat next to me. At the end of the period, I introduced my Chief to the Airman. The Chief asked him (I don't remember his name) if he would teach the entire two weeks. He said, "Yes."

At the beginning of the next period, about a half-dozen instructors joined the class. Two weeks later, I felt confident enough to teach the course.

In May 1965, I passed the examination for promotion to E7, Chief Petty Officer: but the E7

Figure 4: M. Clark, E7, US Navy

AT rating was closed. Simultaneously, the ASW specialization field was becoming so complicated that the Navy, in its infinite wisdom, decided to create a separate AX rating. I was hesitant to consider a rating change because the last time the Navy did this, the program failed.

My Division Officer helped me decide by handing me two special request "chits." One asked for a transfer to the new AX rating; the second, an immediate transfer to the fleet. I didn't want to risk going to an aircraft carrier, so I signed the request to transfer to the AX rating. The transfer came with a nice bonus; promotion to E7, Anti-Submarine Warfare Specialist, Chief Petty Officer.

Patrol Squadron SIX (1966-1969)
Replacement Aircrew Training (03/1966-09/1966)

In March 1966, I received orders to Patrol Squadron SIX (VP-6),[22] NAS Barbers Point, Oahu, Hawaii, via replacement aircrew and SERE training at NAS North Island, San Diego, California, and NAS Moffett Field, Mountain View, California. The fun was about to begin.

We shipped our household goods, and BJ and my son departed for Michigan to stay with family. We would meet the week I graduated from the Aircrew Replacement program at NAS Moffett Field. I boarded a plane to Los Angeles, spent two days with my aunt and uncle (the "Flying Sergeant"), then they drove me to NAS North Island,[23] San Diego, to check-in.

My experiences at North Island were—what can I say?—different from anything I had ever experienced. If you want a new, "out of this world" experience, I recommend Survival Evasion Resistance and Escape (SERE) training.[24] Five of us made it to the safe house. The sixth, a not-too-smart Lieutenant Commander (LCDR), got up and walked across the field to the safe house. In doing so, he exposed us, and we

---

[22] https://en.wikipedia.org/wiki/VP-6.

[23] https://en.wikipedia.org/wiki/Naval_Air_Station_North_Island.

[24] See for example https://www.thebalancecareers.com/navy-sere-training-3356100.

were all captured. We spent the next two days in a prison camp—definitely, something I would recommend avoiding.

From there, it was off to NAS Moffett Field[25] and flight crew training. The training was challenging. My classroom training was extended to include both the acoustic and non-acoustic sensor systems. I also garnered additional time in the air onboard the Lockheed P3A Orion,[26] putting what I was learning in the classroom into practice.

As the 4th of July approached, word got out that a flight had been scheduled to fly to NAS Glenview, Illinois, Selfridge Air Force Base (AFB), Mount Clements, Michigan, and Floyd Bennett Field, Brooklyn, New York. I put my name on the passenger list to get dropped off at Selfridge AFB, about 25 miles from my family's home in Sylvan Lake, Michigan. I would get to see BJ's and my parents one last time before departing for VP-6 at NAS Barbers Point, Hawaii.[27]

Friday, 1 July, arrived. We began to taxi out to the runway for take-off when the control tower notified the pilot that Selfridge AFB had closed their runways for maintenance. A sailor wanting to go to Floyd Bennett Field to spend the weekend with his family in Brooklyn was standing by if there was an available seat. Unable to get dropped off at Selfridge

---

[25] https://en.wikipedia.org/wiki/Moffett_Federal_Airfield.

[26] https://en.wikipedia.org/wiki/Lockheed_P-3_Orion.

[27] https://en.wikipedia.org/wiki/Naval_Air_Station_Barbers_Point.

AFB, I gave my seat to him. Little did I know that that simple act was to save my life.

On Monday, 4 July 1966, the crew were retracing their route back to NAS Moffett Field when their Lockheed P3A Orion crashed in a wooded area outside of Battle Creek, Michigan, with no survivors.

While the flight was listed as a training flight, it technically was what we called a "Geedunk" flight—a flight for the benefit of crew and passengers to spend time enjoying themselves—in this case, visiting and celebrating the 4th of July with family—before shipping out.

There were eight survivors that weekend, the airmen dropped off at NAS Glenview, just north of Chicago, Illinois. I would have been a casualty if I had not given up my seat.

No one knows what caused the plane to crash, only that the aircraft rolled over and spiraled straight down into a wooded field outside of Battle Creek. There were four crew members on the plane at the moment of impact. What transpired during those last few seconds would be pure speculation. But what we know is that something went wrong—very wrong—and four people died that day.

Aircrew Training Complete, Joined VP-6 (10/1966)

Training completed, I was given final orders to Patrol Squadron SIX (VP-6). VP-6 was flying the new Lockheed P3A Orion.

Figure 5: Navy Lockheed Orion aircraft of Patrol Squadron 6
The World-famous Blue Sharks in flight near Oahu, Hawaii
Photo credit: US Navy National Museum of Naval Aviation

I was assigned as squadron Naval Air Training and Operating Procedures Standardization (NATOPS) Instructor/Evaluator on acoustic and non-acoustic ASW systems because of my instructor background. Consequently, rather than being assigned to a specific crew, the Operations Officer would assign me to train and evaluate a different aircrew each week.

BJ and my son arrived, having driven 2,429 miles from Pontiac, Michigan, to Mountain View, California. We spent the night together in a motel across from the main gate at NAS

Moffett Field. The next morning, I picked up my travel orders and checked out. We drove to Oakland, dropped our car off at the shipping terminal, and hitched a Travis Air Force Base ride.

Figure 6: P3C assigned to VP-6 making a turn, displaying armament
Note: Squadron designation on tail not visible
Photo credit: VP6.org

We spent the night in the base hotel, then boarded a Military Air Transport Service (MATS) flight to Hickman Air Force Base, Oahu, Hawaii.

After arriving in Hawaii, we obtained a room at a small hotel in Waipahu, Oahu, about three miles from the base front gate. I checked in at the base and made arrangements for base housing. Two days later, I said my goodbyes to BJ and my son, and I was flown to NAF Adak, Alaska,[28] to join the squadron. For me, it would be a short stay in Adak, as the squadron was finishing up the last month of its six-month deployment when I arrived. However, I did manage to get two flights to the North Pole during my short stay.

I spent the next year training and evaluating crews on new equipment being installed on the P3A. I made several trips to Lockheed Aircraft Corporation in Burbank, California, to familiarize myself with changes being incorporated into the P3B.

Off duty, I spent my time SCUBA diving and getting certified as a PADI[29] Master Instructor, in order to teach SCUBA at the base enlisted swimming pool. I also taught my six-year-old son to SCUBA dive, something his mother was not very happy about.

Figure 7: Diving

My son became quite proficient and loved to demonstrate his abilities to new students. He also became quite

---

[28] https://en.wikipedia.org/wiki/Naval_Air_Facility_Adak.

[29] https://www.padi.com/.

knowledgeable about the various dangerous types of marine life like the venomous Lionfish, Scorpionfish, and Cone shells.

One afternoon, I had gone to get some flashbulbs for a night dive when the base Emergency Room called. BJ answered, and they asked for me. She told them I wasn't there. They were desperate. A young sailor had speared a lionfish, then grabbed it with his hand, and pulled it off the spear. The spines in the fins of the lionfish are highly poisonous and they didn't know how to treat its sting.

My son, overhearing the conversation, told his mother, "Tell them to soak him in a full bathtub of hot water—as hot as he can tolerate—for 30 to 45 minutes until the swelling goes down."

BJ filled me in when I returned, and my son and I went down to the dispensary to check on the patient. He was responding nicely. The doctor told me that my wife was amazing.

I smiled and told him, "Yes, she is, but it was my son who told her what to do." My son was seven, and he had just saved his first life.

The year passed all too quickly, and in December, we began to prepare for our next deployment. On 1 January 1968, we deployed to NAF Naha, Okinawa, Japan.[30] During this deployment, VP-6 participated in Operation Market Time

---

[30] https://en.wikipedia.org/wiki/Naha_Air_Base.

patrols.[31] I made several flights to Tan Son Nhut Air Base[32] and Cam Ranh Bay in Vietnam,[33] evaluating crews flying Operation Market Time patrols. Time on the ground during these missions was pretty much limited to refueling. But it was enough time for the flight crews, including myself, to get exposed to Agent Orange, something that none of us had anticipated.

During this deployment, I also served as the Operations Chief Petty Officer, responsible for the daily flight schedule.

❧

The second fatal accident that I survived occurred on Friday, 5 April 1968, in the South China Sea, near Okinawa. On that flight, there were four survivors and eight fatalities.

On Thursday morning, 4 April 1968, the crew of PC6 landed shortly after 0600, having completed the second 2400 to 0600 flight in a row, the completion of the standard nine-day flight cycle. For the next three days, they would be grounded for some much-needed rest.

The Patrol Plane Commander (PPC), LCDR Dan Jones, stopped by my office about 0800 to verify that his crew was off the flight schedule. He asked if I could take some time off

---

[31] Market Time Patrols meant flying down the South Vietnam coast looking for shipping that were smuggling weapons to the Viet Cong; that is, the ships we were trying to intercept were bringing weapons to market, see Operation Market Time, https://en.wikipedia.org/wiki/Operation_Market_Time. The picture of a VP-40 SP-5B is the same as the ones I flew in Bermuda.

[32] https://en.wikipedia.org/wiki/Tan_Son_Nhut_Air_Base.

[33] https://en.wikipedia.org/wiki/Cam_Ranh_Bay.

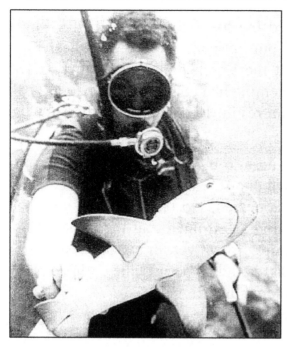

Figure 8: Diving with shark

to go SCUBA diving. I had just finished publishing the flight schedule for the next four days, so I said, "Yes," that I would meet him at the diving locker at 1030.

We had a great dive and returned to the base at about 1630, only to discover that the flight schedule had been changed. LCDR Jones and his crew were back on the flight schedule for the 2400 to 0600, 5 April flight period—a flight that broke virtually every regulation in the book.

First, the crew would exceed the monthly 130-hour flight limitation. Second, the PPC had not only been SCUBA diving in the past 24 hours, but he had also descended to 100 feet and made a controlled ascent, which automatically grounded him for 24 hours to prevent the risk of decompression sickness, i.e., the "bends."

The Commanding Officer (CO) was responsible for the change, seeing an opportunity to get some additional submarine training time with USS Rock transiting the area, and he refused to back down. The crew of PC6, come hell or high water, was going to fly a non-essential training mission.

LCDR Jones invited me to perform a NATOPS Flight Check, and I agreed. I put my name on the call sheet for a 2200 wake-up call: but the watch didn't wake me. LCDR Jones assumed that something had come up: so, he didn't call the barracks either. As a result, I became a survivor for the second time in my life.

I submitted a deposition to the officers investigating the crash, but it was returned unopened. I had put it in the basket on my desk, and it disappeared. No one had seen who had taken it. The investigation determined that the cause of the crash was due to pilot error. However, in my book, the error rested solely on the CO's shoulders because he violated Navy regulations when he ordered that flight.

The remainder of my deployment was routine. Off duty time, I made a few more dives off Suicide Cliff[34]—now Peace Prayer Park—and I made a final visit to the Cave of the Virgins[35] to pay my respects. I flew a couple more Market Time patrols but decided not to reenlist when my enlistment ended the following year. About ten days before the deployment was to end officially, the CO and his crew departed for NAS Barbers Point, leaving the Executive Officer (XO) in charge.

---

[34] https://www.tracesofwar.com/sights/31023/Suicide-Cliff-Okinawa.htm.

[35] See https://fareastfling.me/2014/10/08/okinawan-war-lily-corps-himeyuri-schoolgirls/, https://www.latimes.com/archives/la-xpm-1995-06-04-mn-9231-story.html.

Finally, the deployment ended, and I caught the next to last flight home, looking forward to seeing BJ and my son. They were waiting on the edge of the tarmac when we landed.

The following day, I learned that the squadron XO was now the CO. There had been no change of command ceremony. Nothing. Our CO had departed with no explanation. I would not learn what had happened until 1982 when a friend and former PC-6 crewmember dropped by for a visit. He admitted that he was the one who had walked off with my deposition. He had shared it with the Lockheed representative at NAF Naha, who, I was told, forwarded it to the right people in the chain of command, and the CO was replaced by the XO on 10 May 1968, 10 days before our deployment officially ended.

⤙

The training of flight crews continued until February 1969, when I got into an argument over my not planning to reenlist in May. To make a point of how serious I was, I resigned from flight status.

Fleet Air Wing 2 (FAW-2), to which VP-6 belonged, did not have a qualified NATOPS Instructor/Evaluator for the P3's acoustic and non-acoustic sensor systems or a SERE instructor. A few days before our annual readiness inspection, I received a call to report to the Commander FAW-2. The commander gave me secret orders transferring me to FAW-2 on the morning of the inspection.

At 0500, I received a call from the duty office. The squadron was on ready-alert: all aircraft were launching.

Instead of putting on my uniform, I put on my swim trunks, dive belt, with knife and strap to hold my fins, and grabbed my mask. Ten minutes later, I walked into the office and handed my orders to the Operations Division Officer.

As he began screaming at me, I saluted and said: "Excuse me, Sir, but you have to fly, and I have work to do." With that, I went up to the control tower and told them that when PC-1 (CO) and PC-4 (Personnel Officer) began to taxi out, to call them back.

As I left the control tower, my FAW-2 observer joined me, along with two squads of Marines and four trucks. I gave PC-1's crew to the Marines to drop off on the SERE range at Schofield Barracks. They would attempt to avoid capture, and if caught, be interrogated as prisoners of war.

PC-4 was my project. We loaded them on a truck, with the Marines behind, and headed out to Nānākuli, where they would launch their raft and try to make it down the coast to Makua. The Marines would follow from the road and be prepared to capture them when they made landfall.

The crew started their journey and got about a half-mile offshore when they noticed a destroyer taking part in maneuvers. They fired off some flares and signaled the destroyer with their small survival mirrors. Sure enough, they got the attention of the destroyer, and it launched a whaleboat to investigate.

The FAW-2 observer and I were on surfboards. The destroyer whaleboat crew rescued the plane crew and escorted us back to shore. I found a phone and called FAW-2 to report that I had lost the entire flight crew.

The DO panicked, crying out, "OMG! Sharks got them?"

"No, a destroyer rescued them," I told him.

I wrote my final report and returned to VP-6 to finish out the last days of my military career and settle into our new home in Kaneohe.

Leaving US Navy, Joining Makai Undersea Test Range
(5/1969-9/1970)

My last day in the Navy, 29 May 1969, finally arrived. I woke early, had a light breakfast, and then I drove to squadron headquarters at NAS Barbers Point to pick up my discharge papers. I said my goodbyes and then, made the drive through Honolulu, past Diamond Head and Koko Head, to Waimānalo, and my new job at Makai[36] Undersea Test Range as a saturation diver.[37]

I also began to teach SCUBA after hours. I would spend the next 13 months at Makai Range working on Project AEGIR. After completing AEGIR's first 580-foot dive, my position ended abruptly when the Makai Range [38] CEO announced that they had just filed for bankruptcy.

After that, I continued to teach SCUBA at the Naval Air Station at Barber's Point in Hawaii. I helped my wife get a job with Special Services there. Then, about six months after she got the job as the Assistant to the Director, the Director took medical retirement and my wife was promoted to Director, in effect becoming my boss. Shortly after that, she left me to take care of my son and filed for divorce. When she

---

[36] Makai is Hawaiian and translates "Towards the Sea."

[37] A method of prolonged diving, using an underwater habitat that allows divers to remain in the high-pressure environment of the ocean depths long enough for their body tissues to become saturated with the inert components of the pressurized gas mixture that they breathe, https://www.dictionary.com/browse/saturation-diving.

[38] Makai Range, short for "Makai Undersea Test Range."

came back about a month later, she moved in and asked me to move out. She gained custody of my son during the divorce proceedings. A week after she took on the Director's position, she terminated my contract. A little bit short-sighted on her part, but she wanted me completely out of the picture. She knew that if I didn't have a job teaching on the base, I would have to leave the islands. I stuck it out for about a year playing SCUBA tour guide and then, finally, I took a job with Kentron Hawaii and went to the Kwajalein Missile Range, [39] Kwajalein Atoll, Micronesia.[40]

Figure 9: AEGIR Habitat, Makai Range

---

[39] For background on Kwajalein Missile Range and missile testing at Kwajalein, see http://www.themilitarystandard.com/missile/kwajalein.php, http://articles.latimes.com/1989-03-27/local/me-328_1_star-wars.

[40] Kwajalein Atoll is located in the Republic of the Marshall Islands approximately 2500 miles (5+ hours by air) south and west from Honolulu. The southernmost and largest island in the atoll is named Kwajalein Island, often called by the shortened name, Kwaj, https://en.wikipedia.org/wiki/Kwajalein_Atoll.

The AEGIR habitat, named for the Norse god of the sea, was a fantastic system. It was the first mobile undersea habitat capable of supporting up to six scientists for 14 to 20 days at depths up to 580 feet. Decompression, to prevent decompression sickness,[41] following a saturation dive[42] could take up to seven days, depending on dive depth.

AEGIR consisted of a catamaran[43] hull, three pressurized chambers amidships, consisting of a central sphere for entry and exiting the habitat, and two chambers on either side. The port chamber was the laboratory, and the starboard chamber the living quarters.

---

[41] Decompression sickness (DCS; also known as divers' disease, the bends, aerobullosis, or caisson disease) describes a condition arising from dissolved gases coming out of solution into bubbles inside the body on depressurisation. Decompression of a diver is the reduction in ambient pressure experienced during ascent from depth. It is also the process of elimination of dissolved inert gases from the diver's body, which occurs during the ascent, largely during pauses in the ascent known as decompression stops, and after surfacing until the gas concentrations reach equilibrium, see https://en.wikipedia.org/wiki/Decompression_(diving).

[42] Saturation diving is diving for periods long enough to bring all tissues into equilibrium with the partial pressures of the inert components of the breathing gas. It is a diving technique that allows divers to reduce the risk of decompression sickness ("the bends") when they work at great depths for long periods of time, see https://en.wikipedia.org/wiki/Saturation_diving.

[43] Catamaran is a multi-hulled watercraft featuring two parallel hulls of equal size. It is a geometry-stabilized craft, deriving its stability from its wide beam, rather than from a ballasted keel as with a monohull sailboat, see https://en.wikipedia.org/wiki/Catamaran.

Fore and aft of this central area were variable ballast tanks, with oxygen and helium storage tanks sandwiched between the central chambers and the variable ballast tanks.

In the photo (above), the Emergency Escape Modules (EEM) are missing; however, the forward module's support frame is just to the left of the technician in the white T-shirt. There is an identical frame on the stern. The individual walking towards the center is me.

The dive team would board AEGIR via the central sphere's top hatch. Once onboard, the hatch would be sealed, and the habitat would be pressurized and towed to the dive site. An inspection of the habitat would be made, and then the four bulky lead plugs, one fore and aft on each catamaran hull, would be removed, allowing the hulls to flood.

EMERGENCY ESCAPE MODULE (EEM)

The EEM is a small pressurized vessel capable of carrying up to four divers. Standard procedure, if both EEM were available and operational, was to divide the crew into two groups, with three divers in each EEM.

The EEM, unfortunately, had a maximum depth limitation of 250 feet; consequently, they were unusable at depths greater than 250 feet.

Once onboard the EEM, the hatch was secured, and pressurization initiated, removing all of the water from inside the EEM. The EEM would then release and float to the surface. The rescue vessel would then tow each EEM to the pier, where a crane would pick each one up and mate it with the decompression chamber. The crew would then transfer to the decompression chamber and begin decompression.

Then, water would be slowly pumped into the variable ballast tanks, initiating the descent to the seafloor. The rate of descent could be accurately controlled, allowing for a safe touchdown.

Once on the bottom, the crew could open the bottom hatch and climb down the ladder and swim out through the tunnel created by the catamaran's twin hulls. Because internal habitat pressure equaled outside pressure, there was no need to close the hatch while on the bottom. The crew would seal the bottom hatch at the end of the dive in preparation for the ascent back to the surface.

The nitrogen in the air we breathe causes an intoxicating effect known as nitrogen narcosis[44] or "rapture of the deep." Most divers begin to experience symptoms at depths greater than 100 feet. Nitrogen narcosis is prevented by substituting helium for nitrogen in the breathing mixture.

Helium is not without its adverse effects: its impact on speech can make communication difficult.[45] Under the higher

---

[44] Narcosis while diving (also known as nitrogen narcosis, inert gas narcosis, raptures of the deep, Martini effect) is a reversible alteration in consciousness that occurs while diving at depth. It is caused by the anesthetic effect of certain gases, such as nitrogen, at high pressure. Narcosis produces a state similar to drunkenness (alcohol intoxication), or nitrous oxide inhalation. It can occur during shallow dives but does not usually become noticeable at depths less than 30 meters (100 feet), see https://en.wikipedia.org/wiki/Nitrogen_narcosis.

[45] For an example see Astronaut Scott Carpenter speaking to President Johnson while decompressing in an oxygen-helium atmosphere decompression chamber, see https://www.youtube.com/watch?v=Gg0pMbc7Opk. There is a rather lengthy advertisement at the beginning of the video. The ability to SKIP the majority of the advertisement is active, and we recommend taking advantage of skipping the ad.

pressures that exist in a saturation diving environment, the change in speech becomes even more dynamic, to the point of becoming unintelligible.

During my time at Makai Range, we completed three dives with AEGIR. The first was a 200-foot dive, followed by a 400-foot dive, and, finally, a 580-foot dive. The latter was the final dive.

I was hired for my electronics skills, and the bulk of my time involved maintaining the various electronics systems onboard AEGIR and its support vessel, the *Holokai*.

My relationship with the AEGIR crew was stressful during my first months. They considered me a rank amateur when it came to diving, and I was an outsider. I could never be part of the team in their minds: I was a flyer, not a diver. The fact that I was a certified Professional Association of Diving Instructors (PADI) Master Instructor meant nothing to them.

I had been at Makai Range for about three months when the team's senior divemaster was going through our personnel records, and he found my DD-214N (Record of Service). It showed that I had a secondary Navy Enlisted Classification (NEC) 5345 (SCUBA Diver)—see arrow on figure below.

Once the word spread, attitudes began to change, and I was given more responsibility during diving operations.

Makai Range had a single "Seabird" inflatable boat with a 33-hp Evinrude outboard motor. The Seabird's weakness was a rigid wooden keel, which was continually breaking. I owned a 15-foot Zodiac MK-III Inflatable boat. So, one week,

1. LAST NAME—FIRST NAME—MIDDLE NAME	2. SERVICE NUMBER	
CLARK, JOANNA, MICHELLE	NA	

3. DEPARTMENT, COMPONENT AND BRANCH OR CLASS	3a. GRADE, RATE OR RANK	4. PAY GRADE	5. DATE OF RANK	DAY 16	MONTH MAY	YEAR 65
NAVY --USN	AXC	E-7				

7. U.S CITIZEN	8. PLACE OF BIRTH (City and State or Country)	DATE OF BIRTH	DAY 16	MONTH JUN	YEAR 38
[X] YES [ ] NO	PONTIAC, MICHIGAN				

10a. SELECTIVE SERVICE NUMBER	9. SELECTIVE SERVICE LOCAL BOARD NUMBER, CITY, COUNTY, STATE AND ZIP CODE	DATE INDUCTED DAY MONTH YEAR
		NA

11a. TYPE OF TRANSFER OR DISCHARGE	b. STATION OR INSTALLATION AT WHICH EFFECTED	EFFECTIVE DATE	DAY 19	MONTH MAY	YEAR 69
DISCHARGED	PATROL SQUADRON SIX, NAS, BARBERS POINT, HI				

12. LAST DUTY ASSIGNMENT AND MAJOR COMMAND: PATROL SQUADRON SIX
13a. CHARACTER OF SERVICE: HONORABLE
b. TYPE OF CERTIFICATE ISSUED: DD 256N
14. DISTRICT, AREA COMMAND OR CORPS TO WHICH RESERVIST TRANSFERRED: NOT APPLICABLE
15. REENLISTMENT CODE

16. TERMINAL DATE OF RESERVE/UNIT & S OBLIGATION: NOT APPLICABLE
17. CURRENT ACTIVE SERVICE OTHER THAN BY INDUCTION / SOURCE OF ENTRY: [ ] ENLISTED (First Enlistment) [ ] ENLISTED (Prior Service) [X] REENLISTED [ ] OTHER
18. TERM OF SERVICE: 04
DATE OF ENTRY: DAY 20 MONTH MAY YEAR 65

18. PRIOR REGULAR ENLISTMENTS: 02
19. GRADE, RATE OR RANK AT TIME OF ENTRY INTO CURRENT ACTIVE SVC: AXCA
20. PLACE OF ENTRY INTO CURRENT ACTIVE SERVICE (City and State): MEMPHIS, TENN

21. HOME OF RECORD AT TIME OF ENTRY INTO ACTIVE SERVICE	22. STATEMENT OF SERVICE	YEARS	MONTHS	DAYS
1446 OAKWOOD ST.	(1) NET SERVICE THIS PERIOD	04	00	00
PONTIAC, MICHIGAN	(2) OTHER SERVICE	09	07	08
	(3) TOTAL (Line (1) plus Line (2))	13	07	08
23. SPECIALTY NUMBER & TITLE 5-89.011 DIVER/CONST., SHIP & BOAT BLDG & REP']	b. TOTAL ACTIVE SERVICE	11	10	23
AX-5345	c. FOREIGN AND/OR SEA SERVICE	02	09	00

24. DECORATIONS, MEDALS, BADGES, COMMENDATIONS, CITATIONS AND CAMPAIGN RIBBONS AWARDED OR AUTHORIZED
THIRD GOOD CONDUCT AWARD FOR PERIOD ENDING 26 JUN 67
NATIONAL DEFENSE SERVICE MEDAL
VIET-NAM SERVICE MEDAL   NAVY UNIT COMMENDATION RIBBON

25. EDUCATION AND TRAINING COMPLETED
NTC FOR ABC WARFARE DEFENSE   BEGINNING ALGEBRA I
NTC FOR INTRODUCTION TO SONAR   RADIO SERVICE & REPAIR II
GENERAL OCEANOGRAPHY   INTRODUCTION TO ELECTRONICS II
NAVAL ORIENTATION   PHYSICS II
REVIEW ARITHMETIC   GENERAL SCIENCE I
FUNDAMENTALS OF RADIO   BEGINNING ALGEBRA II   * SEE REMARKS

26a. NON PAY PERIODS/TIME LOST (Preceding Two Years)	b. DAYS ACCRUED LEAVE PAID	27a. INSURANCE IN FORCE (SGLI or USGLI)	b. AMOUNT OF ALLOTMENT	c. MONTH ALLOTMENT DISCONTINUED
TL-NONE	10	[ ] YES [X] NO		

28. VA CLAIM NUMBER: C--
29. SERVICEMEN'S GROUP LIFE INSURANCE COVERAGE: [X] $30,000 [ ] $5,000 [ ] NONE

30. REMARKS
HIGH SCHOOL -04
* AV/B SCHOOL   GENERAL SCIENCE II
  INTERMEDIATE RADIO   INTER COLLEGE ALGEBRA
  RADIO SERVICE & REPAIR I   INTRODUCTION TO ELECTRONICS I

31. PERMANENT ADDRESS FOR MAILING PURPOSES AFTER TRANSFER OR DISCHARGE
45-214 PUALI KOA PLACE
KANEOHE, HAWAII 96744
32. SIGNATURE OF PERSON BEING TRANSFERRED OR DISCHARGED: *Joanna Michele Clark*
33. TYPED NAME, GRADE AND TITLE OF AUTHORIZED OFFICER
T. L. MARTIN
By direction of the Chief of Naval Personnel
34. SIGNATURE OF OFFICER AUTHORIZED TO SIGN: *T. L. Martin*

DD FORM 214N   PREVIOUS EDITIONS OF THIS FORM ARE OBSOLETE.
S/N 0102-003-0260
ARMED FORCES OF THE UNITED STATES
REPORT OF TRANSFER OR DISCHARGE   1

Figure 10: DD214N Record of Service
Note: Name change to Joanna Michelle Clark

I brought it out to the pier. The Zodiac had an inflatable keel. I put a 33-hp Evinrude on it and told the dive team to try it out. They took it into the surf: after 45-minutes, they came back to the pier. They could not stop talking about it. They wanted to replace the Seabird with a Zodiac. Unfortunately, it wasn't in the budget, so I kept mine at the pier for a couple of months.

❧

The first two dives—at 200 and 400 feet—went without a hitch: but the final 580-foot dive was a different story as we came close to losing the entire crew.

The variable ballast system specifications called for a specific type of non-corrosive chromium steel alloy. The contractor built the variable ballast system using regular carbon steel. The result was significant corrosion in the high-pressure air system valves, making it impossible to "blow" the ballast.

The 580-foot dive had been successful up to that point: however, when it came time to blow the variable ballast, nothing happened. The valves had become too corroded, and AEGIR was stuck on the bottom.

The Navy had taken delivery of a Deep Submergence Rescue Vehicle (DSRV-1) on 24 January 1970, but it was not operational yet.

Ghosta Fahlmen, who designed AEGIR, came up with a solution. We ran a hose to the AEGIR, and with a "T" junction, connected it to both catamaran hulls. Then, we pumped helium down, simultaneously displacing the water in both hulls with helium. We used helium rather than air because the expanding helium, being less dense than air, would escape without blowing the hulls apart. We positioned support divers at the outer edge of the expanding gas bubble and waited.

The habitat accelerated on its way up, and, to our surprise, AEGIR came entirely out of the water when it reached the surface, then splashed down. Our support divers jumped onboard and replaced the lead plugs, while two others attached air hoses to the hulls to replace the escaping helium.

The *Holokai* attached a tow cable to the bow and towed the AEGIR back to the pier. The crew locked themselves in the living quarters as we depressurized the laboratory and entry sphere.

Once depressurization was complete, we opened the entry sphere and entered AEGIR. The cleaning crew boarded and cleaned up the laboratory and pantry, then restocked the pantry before closing everything up and repressurizing the laboratory and entry sphere. The crew then moved from the living quarters to the laboratory. Then, we depressurized AEGIR again and cleaned and restocked the living quarters. Finally, we repressurized AEGIR again, restoring the crew's access to all compartments.

The decompression was uneventful, and on the morning of the seventh day, the upper hatch on the center sphere opened and the crew exited AEGIR for the last time. AEGIR was secured, and then we all gathered for debriefing. Following the debriefing, the majority of us received our termination letters.

࿇

The bankruptcy was unfortunate. Tap Pryor, the founder of Sea Life Park, Oceanic Institute, and Makai Undersea Test Range, was a real visionary: but the problem with visionaries is that, sometimes, they're not good business managers. Tap's vision was to create an oceanic center at Makapuu Point. The center would feature an aquarium and educational center for visitors (Sea Life Park), a marine research facility (Oceanic Institute), and a pier and test range for vessels and submersibles (Makai Undersea Test Range). Funding was the problem. The organization was already deeply in debt by the time construction began on Makai Range. They kept robbing money from one program to pay for the next, and they had not paid the rent on the State of Hawaii's property for three years.

As part of the bankruptcy reorganization in 1972, Sea Life Park, Makai Undersea Test Range, and the Oceanic Institute were spun off into separate entities.

The AEGIR habitat was eventually sold and moved to St. Croix, where it was to be the Aquarius' habitat replacement. Unfortunately, funding fell through, and AEGIR was scuttled in 1973.

ॐ

The next morning, I drove into Honolulu to the Employment Development Department (EDD) to file for unemployment. The clerk I drew began the process by asking me if I was hourly or salaried. I told her salaried. She asked if I had any comp time accumulated, and I told her that I had about 230 hours. She asked me if they paid me for those hours, and I said, "No." She picked up her phone and dialed her supervisor.

"I have another one, Clark, with 230 hours," she said.

Then, she finished up my paperwork, told me I would receive $125 a week, and told me to "Go back to Finance at Makai Range and pick up your check for 230 hours of comp time. They owe you $5,060, and they will have it ready for you." I drove back to Makai Range, and my check was waiting for me.

As I thought back over the previous year, I realized that I learned a great deal: but I had to ask myself, "Was it worth it?"

I had rejoined a reserve unit at Barbers Point, but it was going nowhere. There were nine of us, three officers, two chiefs, and four petty officers. We tried to get approval to drill once a month with one of the squadrons at Barbers Point, but our requests went nowhere. Still, it gave me four days of pay ($30 x 4 = $120) for each drill weekend.

I also signed on as a tour guide with South Seas Aquatics in addition to teaching SCUBA at NAS Barbers Point. These two jobs barely gave me enough income to pay the monthly bills. Then, in December, BJ disappeared, leaving my son with me. I had to drop the tourist SCUBA tours to be available to take my son to school in the morning and be there when he came home in the afternoon. BJ returned about three weeks later. She had found a home in Wahiawa, filed for divorce, and the court had awarded her custody and child support. With the child support payments, I could no longer afford what had been our home in Kaneohe.

I finished my final pool session with my last SCUBA class. As I was getting out of the pool, my son was standing there. He wanted his bow and arrow set. I told him he would have to wait until I dismissed the class, which would take about 20 minutes.

BJ's boyfriend was there, and he shouted at me, "You'll get it now!" I released my weight belt and let it drop to poolside: then, he kicked me in the ribs, knocking me backward into the pool. He jumped in on top of me. I could have drowned him, as I had air. But I pushed him away. When he surfaced, he ran from the pool.

My class helped me out of the pool, and I called security. When security arrived, my class verified my story. Unfortunately, I collapsed, and when the medics took me to the dispensary, the x-rays showed two broken ribs. The doctors bound my chest, gave me some antibiotics and pain medication, and let me go home after three hours of observation.

The following weekend, my class graduated, and I certified them as SCUBA divers. They bought all of my equipment at a nice discount. On Monday, I reported to the Captain's office for a Captain's Mast.[46] BJ's boyfriend was charged with assault, fined, and transferred to Japan for a six-month cooling-off period. The Captain thanked me for all I had done teaching SCUBA, and he wished me well on my next journey.

I had accepted a position with Kentron Hawaii, on Kwajalein Atoll, Republic of the Marshall Islands. On 15 March, a friend drove me to Hickam AFB, where I boarded an Air Micronesia charter flight to Kwajalein Atoll. A new chapter in my life was about to begin.

---

[46] A Captain's Mast is a trial where the Captain is judge and jury.

Kwajalein Missile Range, Kwajalein Atoll, Republic of the Marshall Islands (3/1971-12/1972)

I was still in the Naval Reserve, drilling at NAS Barbers Point when my layoff occurred. I felt I could survive for a while, but my situation worsened when my contract teaching SCUBA at NAS Barbers Point abruptly got canceled; an action initiated by BJ.

My XO suggested I could get a job at the Kwajalein Missile Range if I were interested.

I asked, "What would I be doing there?"

"I can get you a job working in one of the electronics shops there," he replied. "It would be an 18-month contract, and you would have the option of extending if you like it there."

I said, "Ok, what do I have to do?"

He made a phone call, then said, "Go down to Kentron Hawaii, Ltd tomorrow morning at 1000 hrs. Ask for Personnel, and tell them I sent you."

The next morning, I checked in with the Personnel Department, filled out a ton of forms, and I was handed a plane ticket. You leave Monday morning. Be at the Hickam AFB terminal at 0530. You will be taking the Air Micronesia (Air 'Mike') flight to Kwajalein Atoll."

Monday morning, I boarded the Air "Mike" flight at Hickam AFB, and three hours later, I arrived on Kwajalein. My new co-workers picked me up at the terminal and transported me to the Sands, which would be my home away from home for the next 21 months.

We dropped my luggage off in my new quarters, then went over to the Yokwe (Senior Staff Dining Hall) for lunch. After lunch, I received an orientation drive: post office, Bank of Hawaii, barber shop, Macy's (PX), main pier, and marine electronics shop, etc.

Our last stop was Kentron Hawaii's main office, where I met my new bosses, Bob Gray and Ed Colburn. I would spend the next week working in the central electronics shop while I familiarized myself with the equipment I would be maintaining. Additionally, my orientation would continue through the remainder of the week.

The following week, I received word that Ed Colburn wanted to see me. I went over to his office, told his secretary who I was, and that Ed wanted to see me. She buzzed his office, and he replied, "Send him in."

Ed shook my hand and thanked me for coming. He then asked, "Do you have professional diving experience?"

I said, "Yes, I am a qualified Navy diver and I worked at Makai Range in Hawaii as a saturation diver."

He asked, "How do you feel about laying undersea cable? The engineer who was going to coordinate the laying of undersea cables in the lagoon has quit. We need someone to take his place. Have you ever been involved in laying undersea cables?"

I said, "I have only been involved in one cable laying operation, and I can't say that it was really heavy involvement. We just went out and scoured the bottom and found a safe place to bring the cable in. But I was not the supervisor."

He said, "That is good enough. You can read books in the library and learn what you need to know to map the bottom of the lagoon and lay the cables."

"The first thing you will need to do is survey the lagoon bottom and map the routes. We need to lay three cables: Kwajalein to Meck, Illeginni to Meck, and Illeginni to Roi-Namur."

"Well," I replied, "We'll need a side-scan SONAR [47] system and a navigation system to plot the route and lay the cable."

Ed responded, "Global will be providing the equipment and operators. They are using a Decca Navigation System for route plotting. Your job will be to coordinate the operation with Art Delacruz, Global's project manager."

So, I got a promotion to be the Project Coordinator, which brought me from a $3.50 an hour job to a $4.20 an hour supervisory job. I also had free room and board and free medical, so actually I was being well paid. All I had to spend my money on was keeping myself in a pair of shorts and a

---

[47] Side-scan uses a sonar device that emits conical or fan-shaped pulses down toward the seafloor across a wide angle perpendicular to the path of the sensor through the water, which may be towed from a surface vessel or submarine or mounted on the ship's hull. The intensity of the acoustic reflections from the seafloor of this fan-shaped beam is recorded in a series of cross-track slices. When stitched together along the direction of motion, these slices form an image of the sea bottom within the swath (coverage width) of the beam. The sound frequencies used in side-scan sonar usually range from 100 to 500 kHz; higher frequencies yield better resolution but less range. See: https://en.wikipedia.org/wiki/Side-scan_sonar.

tee-shirt because that is what everybody wore. Most of the time, I was out on the barge laying cable or doing mapping: so, I was usually wearing bathing trunks, shower shoes, and a tee-shirt. I was there from March of 1971 to December of 1972, just about 22 months.

ھ

I met with Art Delacruz that afternoon, and he brought me up to speed on where the project stood at the moment. I spent the next week in the Bell Laboratories technical library, getting up to speed on Decca navigation and its accuracy. The following week Art and I enlisted a Huey (UH-1 Helicopter). We flew to Meck, Illeginni, and Roi-Namur to see how construction on the cable landing sites was progressing.

Art then set out to configure a tugboat to launch, tow, and recover the side-scan sonar on the stern. He also installed and configured the bridge's Decca navigation system.

We decided to do Illeginni to Roi-Namur first. We started with a visual surface scan identifying major coral heads, then followed up with side-scan sonar to determine the cable's best route. We repeated the process with the Illeginni to Meck route and finished with the Kwajalein to Meck route. We were ready to lay our cables. All we needed now was the cable, but its delivery was behind schedule.

In the meantime, the development of the Safeguard and Sprint anti-ballistic missile (ABM) system[48] continued with

---

[48] Safeguard/Sprint ABM Program. See
https://en.wikipedia.org/wiki/Safeguard_Program.

the launch of a Sprint missile.[49,] The launch was unbelievable as it accelerated to Mach 10—more than 7,600 miles per hour—within seconds of its launch.[50]

The cables finally arrived, and the installation began. The installations of the Illeginni to Meck and Illeginni to Roi-Namur cables were successful. We ran into a snag with the Kwajalein to Meck cable, however. The Soviet Union and the United States signed the Strategic Arms Limitation Treaty (SALT) on 26 May 1972. We were not only underway, we were also less than 100 yards from the Meck drop-off point when the order came to abandon the cable and return to Kwajalein. The cable cost approximately $25 million: so, we decided to seal the end and push it into the termination box and seal it. To activate the cable, they would only have to remove the cable from the termination box, clean out the sealant, and pull it into the building on Meck.

When we got back to Kwajalein, I reported what we had done. Upper management went ballistic.

---

[49] Sprint was a two-stage, solid-fuel anti-ballistic missile (ABM), armed with a W66 enhanced-radiation thermonuclear warhead used by the United States Army. It was designed to intercept incoming reentry vehicles (RV) after they had descended below an altitude of about 60 kilometres (37 miles), where the thickening air stripped away any decoys or radar reflectors and exposed the RV to observation by radar. As the RV would be travelling at about 5 miles (8.0 km) per second, Sprint had to have phenomenal performance to achieve an interception in the few seconds before the RV reached its target. See https://en.wikipedia.org/wiki/Sprint_(missile).

[50] Sprint salvo launch 17 March 1971 Kwajalein. Two Sprints launched less than 1 second apart intercepted a Minuteman I RV launched from Vandenberg. See http://www.nuclearabms.info/Sprint.html.

I told them, "Look, it is not usable, and it is not accessible from inside the control center. The end of the cable is just secure and safe should the cable ever be needed in the future."

࿇

Two incidents occurred during the following month that made for a good laugh. I spent all my off-duty time diving the numerous World War II wrecks in the Kwajalein lagoon and taking pictures. I also had a dispute with the Range Safety office. They would not approve my SCUBA course curriculum unless I dropped "emergency swimming ascents" from the curriculum. Consequently, I refused to teach and certify students. You might say my relationship with the Range Safety was non-existent.

I was in Macy's one afternoon picking up a 15-mm Nikon wide-angle lens. At the counter, a gentleman next to me commented on the lens and asked if I was a diver.

I said, "Yes."

He said, "Me too. I just wish I had time to make a couple of dives while I'm here." Then, he introduced himself. "I'm Brigadier General Flanagan, by the way."

The General ran the Safeguard program, and he was on an inspection tour of the facilities. I told him I would have to clear it with Range Safety, but a group of us were making a night dive that evening. We had reserved a boat for an ocean dive on Saturday, the next day, as well. The General said he would have to change his schedule, but he would like to join us for both dives.

I said, "I'll make the call."

I called Range Safety, identified myself, and I asked to speak to the Colonel.

The Captain asked, "About what?"

I replied, "It's personal."

We went back and forth until, clearly frustrated, he put me through to the Colonel. The Colonel was not in a good mood.

"What's so personal that you need to talk to me?"

I replied, "Colonel, I have a friend visiting the island for a few days. He is an NAUI certified diver, and he would like to join us tonight and tomorrow for a wreck and open-ocean dive. I will take responsibility for him."

The Colonel replied, "No. You know the rules."

"Yes, Colonel," I said, "I know your rules, but I don't think you will be pleased if he has to call you."

"Let him call me," the Colonel replied.

"Ok, I'll tell the General to call you directly."

That got his attention. "General?"

"Yes, my friend is Brigadier General Flanagan, and he wants to go diving with us."

The Colonel decided it was in his best interest to approve my request.

❧

The second incident occurred during an open-ocean survey off of Meck. We were scanning the ocean bottom in about 6,000 feet of water, looking for a location to plant a hydrophone to register open-ocean RV impacts.

We were scanning an area about five miles square. It was nighttime when the tugboat captain noticed we were being tracked by another vessel. When the sun came up, we saw that the ship that was tracking us was a Soviet trawler. The tugboat captain suggested we help them with their boredom. The tug had an abundant supply of sex magazines—Playboy, Playgirl, Hustler. He told the crew to gather them up, tie them together, and attach the package to a large fishing pole.

Then, the tugboat captain headed for the Soviet trawler. As we pulled alongside, the crew passed the package over to the Soviet crew. As we started to pull away, the Soviet crew waved us back and passed us a gallon bottle of vodka. I stood on the bow taking pictures of the Soviet vessel, failing to notice that two Army helicopters were circling overhead.

That afternoon, we pulled into the pier on Kwajalein. Waiting for us was the base commander, Global management, and my bosses. They were not happy: but their anger gradually turned to laughter as they climbed into their vehicles and headed back to their office with our bottle of vodka. Besides, they gained some valuable intel because I had gotten close-up photos of all the antennas and other equipment.

ॐ

When I went to Kwaj, I came back to visit every six months. Hawaii required a six-month waiting period to finalize my divorce from BJ: the initial divorce was granted and then six months later, it was finalized. I left for Kwaj three months into the divorce process. The first time I came back to Hawaii, my son wasn't there. BJ took off and disappeared with him. I had to go to court and tell them, "I can only come in once every six months and I want to see my son." The next time, she had a court order that said that I was to be able to see him. So, I got to see him from eight o'clock in the morning until five o'clock at night on the Saturday and Sunday when I was there. And that was it—once every six months.

The next time I came in, I thought my son and I had a good time. We went SCUBA diving and he said he wanted to learn how to fly an airplane. So, I took him flying. I gave him two hours of flight instruction. I waited on the ground while he went up with the instructor. When they came back, he was all ecstatic about his flight. He was just bubbling over, "I had so much fun. Thank you, thank you, thank you."

On Monday morning, when I was at the airport, I called to say goodbye to him, and his mother told me that he was already on his way to school. Then, a week after I was back on Kwaj, I got the letter that said I was standing in the way of his happiness and that he wanted to be adopted by his mom's new husband.

The psychologist on the base in Kwaj looked at the letter and said, "An eleven-year-old boy didn't write this."

I said, "I know."

But the psychologist said, "The reality is you can't bring him out here, even if you had custody. If you stay in his life, he is probably going to be destroyed."

So, I bit the bullet and agreed to the adoption. After that, I did not see or hear from him for 33 years. I think that contributed to my crisis in Hawaii because in a way, my son was my anchor. Once he was born, I couldn't even think about going through gender change. I simply couldn't. I had a responsibility and I had to fulfill that responsibility in the best way that I could—which wasn't very good. I did support him but there were times that I should have been there for him; but I wasn't. It wasn't an easy situation.

స

I met Sally[51] shortly after the beginning of my divorce. She was living in Honolulu and I was living in Kaneohe on the other side of the island. I initially had no real romantic interest in her, but she was a SCUBA diver, and she became my diving partner. We dove together two to three times a week until I left for Kwaj. One time when I came in from Kwaj, we went over to the big island to a diving lodge and spent the weekend diving. She wanted to get married, and I was having real difficulties with that.

When I came for another week, we planned to go to the mainland to visit my folks and then on to Chicago to meet Sally's folks. It was her idea because she really wanted to get married. But I made an excuse that I couldn't go, that I had to leave and go back to Kwaj on Monday. She had her tickets already, so she made the trip without me and I took the plane back to Kwaj. When I think back on it, I know it sounds like it was all her fault. There was a little bit of pressure there. She wanted to get married. But if it hadn't been for my gender issues, I would have married her right away. I would have said, "Let's go do it" because she was fun, and she was a SCUBA diver. At the time, I was having more and more problems with my gender issues. We exchanged a couple of letters after that, but I was slow responding to her and the last

---

[51] A pseudonym.

letter I got from her she said, "You must be really busy because I haven't heard from you."

My next trip to Honolulu in October 1972 was for business. I flew to Honolulu to go over my reports and interpret the Decca navigation data showing where present and past cables were laid. At that point, I had known Jessica[52] for about six months. She was the secretary for my counterpart in Honolulu. We mostly talked on the phone and most of the time, it was just about business. Sometimes, I would ask, "How are you doing?" and we would talk about little personal things. I saw Jessica whenever I was in Honolulu to see my counterpart and, occasionally, I would take her out to lunch. But we didn't start a relationship until I came in from Kwaj the next time.

She had arranged a hotel room and rental car for me, and I had told her that I would give her a ride home after I got cleaned up. I was going to take her out to dinner. But when I stepped out of the shower, got dressed, and came out of the bathroom, she was sitting there waiting. The sunlight was shining through the window onto her hair and I just looked at her and said, "We should get married." She turned and looked at me in surprise and said, "Ok."

If there was something subconscious in my mind when I asked her to marry me, I don't know what it was. I just walked out, looked at her, and said, "We should get married." It just popped out. Then I was thinking to myself, "Oh my God. What did I just do?" I wasn't even thinking about it when I walked out of the bathroom. That was the last thing on my mind. I had no intention of asking her to marry me—or so I thought—but there I was, proposing on the spur of the

---

[52] A pseudonym.

moment. I just blurted it out. Then I thought, *What am I doing? What am I saying?* But it was too late, she had already said yes. The next morning, we found a judge and got married. We spent the weekend on the Big Island, getting back in time for me to catch my Monday morning flight back to Kwajalein.

The bottom line is we both benefitted from the marriage. I got her to a doctor to clean up her acne—she had the worst acne I had ever seen; even the doctor said, "Wow!"—and she still had her braces on her teeth from when she was twelve. She was terrified of doctors, so getting that taken care of was a good thing for her because she was quite beautiful—especially after the acne went away and we got the braces off her teeth—and she had a wonderful personality. Without that, she may have never married anybody because I don't think she had even dated anyone. On the other hand, I doubt if I would be here today if it hadn't been for her.

I still had six months to go in Kwaj, so Jessica stayed in Hawaii. It was on the next trip when I came back in December that we ran into Sally. Jessica picked me up at the airport and we stopped at the Ala Moana Shopping Center to get some clothes for me. When we got out of the car and walked around the corner of the building from the parking space, there was Sally. We ran right into her. I had written to her to say that I had gotten married, but she was devastated.

It wasn't until I was in transition that I wrote her again and told her, "It wasn't you. It was me and here's where I am now."

She wrote back, "Oh my God! Now I understand."

And we have been friends ever since.

ॐ

In December 1972, my tour with Kentron Hawaii, on Kwajalein, ended with the signing of the Salt Agreement— the strategic arms treaty between the United States and Russia.[53] After that, there was no more cable laying to be done. The US cancelled the program immediately. I was offered a job in Calgary, Canada, but Jessica didn't want to go to Calgary. I didn't really want to go there either. I couldn't find full-time work. So, I returned to Honolulu, my marriage, and the Naval Reserve. My former reserve unit had been dis-established, so I joined a unit at Commander-in-Chief Pacific Fleet (CINCPACFLT). I went back to teaching SCUBA diving in Hawaii on a part-time basis and went to college on the GI bill.[54] That way, we were able to make ends meet while I continued to look for a job.

But that is when I started to unravel. All of my crutches were gone, and my struggle over my gender resurfaced. I needed help but didn't know where to turn. I had enrolled at Leeward College, but it didn't keep me busy enough and my son asking to be adopted made it clear I would never see him again.

---

[53] Agreements, known as SALT I and SALT II, were signed by the United States and the Union of Soviet Socialist Republics (USSR) in 1972 and 1979, respectively, intended to end the arms race in strategic, long-range or intercontinental, ballistic missiles armed with nuclear weapons, https://www.britannica.com/event/Strategic-Arms-Limitation-Talks.

[54] The Servicemen's Readjustment Act, 1944 was created to help veterans of WWII offering low-interest mortgages and stipends to cover tuition for college or trade schools, https://www.history.com/topics/world-war-ii/gi-bill.

By late January 1973, Jessica and I had been married about 18 months when I made the suicide attempt. She stopped me by kicking the knife out of my hand. She had been taking karate. She was a tall woman, almost as tall as me. She tossed me into the car and took me to the mental health crisis center. For the first time, I was able to tell a doctor what was going on. He said, "You need to go to Stanford." So, we filed for divorce—actually, I went and filed for divorce because she couldn't take the time off from work.

The judge asked, "You are not employed. Do you want support?"

I said, "No, I do not want support. We still love each other but not enough to be married. It just didn't work out."

So, he signed the divorce. By that time, the divorce could be finalized right away. Jessica stood by me over the next month while we tied things up in Honolulu so that I could leave.

My journey was about to take another turn. This time, a positive one.

Transition Finally Arrives

My transition, you could say, began with my suicide attempt. Had it not been for Jessica, I would not be here today. She physically stopped me, then took me to the crisis center, where I was able to talk openly about my gender conflict for the first time in my life. After much discussion, the doctor suggested I relocate to the mainland[55] since my son was still living on the Island. He recommended I consider the Stanford Gender Program.

Over the next couple of weeks, I tied up loose ends and got ready to leave. Jessica called my parents and put me on the phone with them. My tickets to come back to the States, routed me to San Francisco through Los Angeles. I didn't know what I was going to do when I got to San Francisco. I only had a few hundred dollars to my name.

Two days later, Jessica drove me to the airport. She called my parents again as soon as I was on the plane, gave them my flight number and arrival time in Los Angeles, and told them that I would be changing planes to fly to San Francisco.

She said, "You better meet the plane because I don't know what will happen after that."

I had an hour layover before going on to San Francisco and that is when my parents found me and said, "Come on. You are coming home with us." What I did not know at the

---

[55] Hawaiian reference for the 48 contiguous states.

time was that after they talked to Jessica, they went and saw a psychiatrist to find out what was going on.

The doctor said, "I don't know a whole lot about it except that if your child is a transsexual"—at that time the word transgender didn't exist[56] —"then your son is your daughter and you had better get used to the idea. Otherwise, your daughter will most likely commit suicide."

Dad said, "Well, she has already tried it once."

I was unaware that they had taken it upon themselves to visit a psychiatrist to learn as much as they could about what I was experiencing. I initially resisted the suggestion that I come home with them, but then Mom told me they had seen a psychiatrist, and he had recommended the Stanford Program. I had not mentioned the Stanford Gender Program to them, so I felt that they were not judging me to be crazy: rather, they truly wanted to help.

I had flown home in male attire, as I was far too afraid to attempt traveling in female attire. But when we got home, I unpacked and changed. I had brought some female clothing with me that Jessica had helped me to buy. I put on a dress, and nervously stepped out into the family room where Mom and Dad were waiting.

---

[56] Transsexual was the original definition coined by Harry Benjamin, M.D. It has been replaced by "transgender," which is inaccurate. The individual suffering from gender identity conflict, changes their sex to conform to their gender identity. They do not change their gender, as the term transgender implies.

I told them, "This is how I have felt all of my life. From now on, this is the way it is going to be. I am sorry."

With that, my dad handed me a paper sack with three pairs of nylons in it. I always laugh when I tell this part of the story.

↝

My mother had a much more difficult time with my transition. It wasn't that she was negative about it herself. It was that her mother was. My grandmother was just as hostile as can be. She was fit to be tied. She was not the least bit accepting, and she had no interest in learning what I was going through. My grandmother refused to call me Joanna, nor would she use female pronouns. The norm was that she'd raise her voice in anger and ask, "Do you know what you're doing to your parents."

My grandmother was paralyzed on her left side, the result of a brain aneurysm that she had while in her 60s. My uncle, the "Flying Sergeant," and his wife lived in Costa Mesa, and Grandma would spend two weeks with them and then come to stay with my parents for two weeks. When she stayed with us (approximately every two weeks), I would move out of my bedroom into the living room to make room for Grandma and do my best to keep out of the way.

Mom's only relief was to visit the neighbors, Charley, and June Straumer. Charley was the cinematographer for the 1959 movie *The Untouchables,*[57] and they had some familiarity

---

[57] Originally a tv series (1959-1963),
https://www.imdb.com/title/tt0052522/, later released as a movie
(1987), https://www.imdb.com/title/tt0094226/.

with transsexual people in Hollywood. They understood what Mom and I were going through. They were a Godsend for both of us. My mom spent a lot of time over there talking with them. They told her what they knew from Hollywood and, for the most part, my mom went along with it. She even made some dresses for me that fit. She was a great seamstress, although some of the dresses I didn't really like. They were very flowery. I thought, *I have to wear this to work? Oh, God! They will see me from a mile away.*

I began to get comfortable in my new identity, and I wrote to the Stanford Gender Program seeking an appointment. It came through, and Mom and Dad drove me to Palo Alto. I met Drs. Laub and Fisk, and they accepted me into the program for the "real-life test," which required that I live and function as a member of the female gender for the next two years.

There wasn't much of a transsexual community in the 1970s. I met my first transsexuals when I was accepted into the Stanford Gender Program. While I found the female-to-male (FtM) clients to be a relatively close-knit group, the male-to-female (MtF) clients were not.

The Stanford Gender Program had a half-way house run by an FtM and his wife. At any one time, about five MtF individuals stayed there, but they never socialized outside of the home. I stayed at the house for about three months until I finally found a full-time job as a secretary in Mountain View with Traffic Safety Research (TSR).

In comparison to the other MtF people who I met early on, my transition was relatively smooth. The most significant difference was that I had my parents' support, while the others had experienced rejection rather than love.

During my stay at the half-way house, I changed my name legally to Joanna Michelle Clark. Social Security changed my name, but not my gender, on my records. Thanks to the Stanford Gender Program's efforts, the California Department of Motor Vehicles (DMV) issued me a new license with my name and gender corrected.

TSR was my first full-time job after beginning transition. Near the end of my time with TSR, they agreed to join with another company to bid on a saturation diving project, something they were ill-equipped to do. It was my job to type up their proposals, and it was clear they had no idea what they were doing.

One morning, I picked up the draft proposal and walked into the engineering office, and asked, "What do you think you're doing? You're insane if you think you'll get the contract with this. It's clear you don't know the first thing about saturation diving."

One of the engineers came back with a sexist remark, "And what do you think you know about saturation diving? You're a woman."

I responded, "First, I'm a qualified Navy diver. Second, I've trained as a saturation diver, and third, I'm also a certified master instructor in Self-Contained Underwater Breathing Apparatus (SCUBA)."

That brought another round of sexist remarks indicating disbelief, drawing the boss into the room. He ended the discussion by declaring, "What she said is true. So, you might listen to her."

I rewrote the proposal, and we submitted it. In the meantime, I finally received a response from the Navy.

They were not very cooperative, however. The Navy gave me an Honorable Discharge from the Naval Reserve, but it had a RE-4 (Ineligible for Reenlistment) Code, and they refused to update my name and gender. That was going to make it impossible to find employment that complimented my skills.

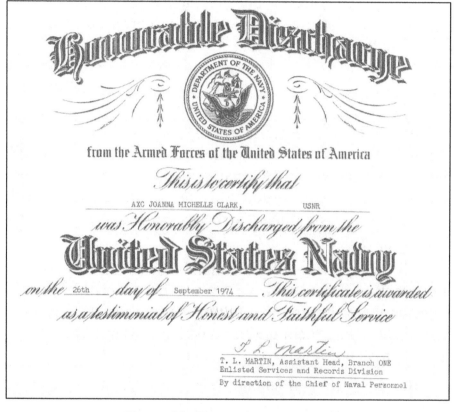

Figure 11: Honorable Discharge
Note: Name change to Joanna Michelle Clark

I wrote letters to my Representative Patsy Mink (D-HI) and Senator Philip Hart (D-MI), my father's friend. The Navy told Representative Mink, "No."

They said, "Yes," to Senator Hart, however.

An aide to Senator Hart told my father that the Navy had initially said, "No," but, allegedly, when the Senator told them he would not schedule appropriation hearings for their new aircraft carrier until my records were corrected, they capitulated. A few weeks later, I received a large envelope from the Navy Department containing my corrected DD-256N and DD-214N for all three active-duty enlistments. I learned later that the Navy had issued corrected records at least four times previously.

❧

At TSR, the response to my proposal finally came through. It wasn't accepted, and a month later, the layoffs began. Eventually, TSR closed its doors. Once again, I was unemployed, and I had no choice but to move back in with my parents. I was fortunate in this aspect because my parents were supportive.

My surgery was still nine months away. At this point in my transition, my experience was that the majority of parents rejected their children by simply shutting the door in their faces and telling them not to come back. Many MtF people ended up on the streets.

Before I left Mountain View, the Stanford Gender Program scheduled a parent's night to help parents better understand what their children were going through. On the night of the meeting, there were about 70 patients present. Most were MtF people, with a handful of FtM individuals. I was the only patient accompanied by parents.

After Dad listened to the other patient's stories, he volunteered to write letters to their parents, saying, "I've met your child, and she is a wonderful person. You should get to know her because it isn't her fault that she is going through this."

My father became quite an advocate over the next couple of years.

If I recall correctly, Dad only received a single response. The family said, "Don't write to us again," but it didn't stop him. He kept writing letters for those in need.

In the 1970s, there was not a lot of medical or scientific evidence regarding what caused gender identity conflict or gender dysphoria as it has become more widely known. Most early researchers believed that the underlying cause was nurture, that it was a choice. More recent research indicates that MtF people's brain structure, with early-onset gender dysphoria, is similar to the brain structure of cisgender[58] women and unlike that of cisgender men.[59] [60]

---

[58] Cisgender is a term for people whose gender identity matches the sex that they were assigned at birth. For example, someone who identifies as a woman and was assigned female at birth is a cisgender woman. The term *cisgender* is the opposite of the word *transgender*. See https://en.wikipedia.org/wiki/Cisgender.

[59] The largest study involving transgender people is providing long-sought insights about their health. See https://www.nature.com/articles/d41586-019-01237-z.

[60] A significant association was identified between gender dysphoria and ERα, SRD5A2, and STS alleles, as well as ERα and SULT2A1 genotypes. Several allele combinations were also overrepresented in transgender women, most involving AR (namely, AR-ERβ, AR-PGR, AR-COMT, CYP17-SRD5A2). Overrepresented alleles and genotypes

֍

Upon returning to my parent's home, I enrolled at Saddleback College under the GI Bill, but my initial experience was hostility when the restrooms were declared off-limits. Not knowing my next career, I enrolled in a testing program, taking a battery of psychological and vocational attitude examinations to determine my interests and abilities. The test results were earth-shattering. I was best suited to be:

1) Catholic Nun school teacher,

2) Catholic Nun counselor, or

3) civil and human rights attorney.

I also enrolled in a human sexuality course at the University of California—Irvine (UCI). It was here that I met Jude Patton, an FtM guest speaker and trans-activist. I had had so few problems in my transition that I had not given a second thought to becoming a political activist or a trans-activist for that matter. That was about to change.

Jude had created the Renaissance Newsletter and Renaissance Gender Identity Services, and I became involved in that enterprise with him.

I was enrolled in a course called "Human Services through Legislation" at Saddleback College. My professor gave us Saul Alinsky's book *Rules for Radicals: A Pragmatic*

---

are proposed to under-masculinize/feminize on the basis of their reported effects in other disease contexts. See https://pubmed.ncbi.nlm.nih.gov/30247609/.

Primer for Realistic Radicals as a reading assignment. I was being primed: I just didn't know it.

☙

I managed to obtain a job in March 1975 with the County of Orange Environmental Management Agency as a clerk-typist through the Comprehensive Employment and Training Act (CETA) Program. The best part was that the job included Prudential Health Insurance. Prudential was the only insurance company that would pay for sex-reassignment surgery (SRS).

Figure 12: Joanna

My medical benefits became active in mid-June, and I told my supervisor that my doctor said I needed a hysterectomy. She approved my sick-leave, and I prepared to fly to Oklahoma City for SRS. I had completed my studies for the semester at UCI and Saddleback College during the first week of June. On 22 June 1975, I flew to Oklahoma City and underwent SRS two days later, on the 24th.

I returned home a week later, after a successful surgery. My grandmother was supposed to be staying in Costa Mesa for the next two weeks. I went into the bedroom and was lying on the bed, changing my bandages, when my grandmother rolled into the doorway in her wheelchair. My uncle Kelly and Aunt Lila were curious, as was my grandmother, so they came to visit unannounced.

The master bedroom with its bathroom was my grandmother's whenever she was visiting. Due to her brain aneurysm, she was partially paralyzed on her left side and relied on a wheelchair. She had a floor-to-ceiling bar in the bathroom that allowed her to pull herself onto the toilet and then swing herself back into her wheelchair when finished.

She came down the hallway in her wheelchair and stopped in the doorway, staring. I was lying on the bed, changing a dressing, and she just sat there and stared. My mother came up behind her, and when my grandmother told her she needed to use the bathroom, I looked up and told her, "Go ahead, Grandma."

My grandmother rolled herself into the bathroom. A few minutes later, I heard the toilet flush, and she moved back into the bathroom doorway and resumed her staring.

I looked up and asked both of them, "Do you want to look?"

I couldn't believe how fast those two moved! My grandmother got to my bedside first, looked at me, then looked up at my mother, and said, "She looks just like us."

That was the first time she'd ever used the female pronoun. In the weeks that followed, my grandmother became supportive. More importantly, she made it clear to everyone that I was her granddaughter.

☙

I returned to work four weeks later to a real surprise. I was no longer a clerk typist: I was now the Office Supervisor. Things went well on the job over the next four months with few complaints, although one staff complained about a new CETA employee who was doing poorly as a file clerk. I went into the file room and observed her for a short time, then walked over and asked her if she could read a document. I realized that she couldn't do her job properly because she had poor eyesight. I asked her where her glasses were, and she told me she didn't have glasses because she couldn't afford them.

Figure 9: Jude Patton and Joanna

One of the benefits of being a CETA employee was assistance with health issues that interfered with one's ability to work. I took her down to Personnel, and they arranged for her to get an eye examination and glasses. She became one of our best employees and later transferred from CETA to full employee status.

☙

About this time, my new friend Jude Patton, knowing I was studying to become a social worker, invited me to go with him to visit the Melrose-Wilcox Mental Health Center in Los Angeles. Ar'lene Lafferty had created a support group for transsexuals there, and Jude had concerns about a doctor, John R. Brown, who was preying on MtF patients, some of whom were members of this group. I agreed to go with him, unaware that this would become a significant turning point in my life.

There were about 15 MtF clients there, and they all had a common complaint. They could not find jobs because of their birth certificates. I somehow doubted this because not once had I ever been asked for my birth certificate.

I responded, "I don't understand. Why can't you change your birth certificate?"

More than one replied, "California's Department of Vital Records will not change name and gender on birth records."

I was born in Michigan, and I had not given any thought to changing my birth certificate.

I asked why they refused, and again the group responded, "The law doesn't permit it."

I replied, "Then change the law."

That did not sit well with many of them, and it became clear they were uncomfortable having me there.

On the trip home, Jude and I discussed what had happened. I had never been any sort of activist. I seldom voted, and up to that point, the first and last time I had voted was in 1960 for John F. Kennedy, even though I considered myself to be a Republican.

By the time we got home, I had decided I would try to change the law. I was going to be not only a trans-activist but a political activist.

I had spent my entire adult life defending the Constitution, and I had recited our Pledge of Allegiance more times than I could remember.

One phrase that had always stuck with me was "One nation, indivisible, with liberty and justice for all." But now, for the first time in my life, I was beginning to realize that this was not true. It was just one of those "feel good" pledges forced on us as children so that we would not notice the untruths of the phrase "liberty and justice for all." The phrase applied to men only—white men, that is.

The next morning, I went to work early. Using one of the Lexitron word processors in our office, I wrote a letter. I ran off 120 individually addressed letters to each member of our state legislature, calling for a change in the birth certificate law to permit a change in name and gender. I was now officially a trans activist. I planned to sign and mail the letters after I got home. But, for now, it was back to work.

Over the next month, I received a total of ten response letters. Most said, "Thank you for your message, but I am unable to assist." Then, out of the blue, I received a call from Paul Perdue, a San Francisco attorney. He had a client he was trying to assist in getting her birth certificate changed, and he had seen my letter. He had a friend who might help. Two weeks later, I received a letter from the Speaker of the Assembly, Willie Brown. He was introducing AB-385 to change the law so that birth certificates could be corrected. Eighteen months and a dozen trips to Sacramento to lobby and testify, and AB-385 was signed into law, effective 1 January 1978.

&

In the meantime, I spent the bulk of my days running the Environmental Management Agency clerical support services. We had a large Xerox copier in our documents room, and we would print as many as a hundred copies of multipage documents every week. Then, we had to collate them by hand in preparation for binding. Collating by hand was a time-consuming and costly exercise. I submitted a proposal to purchase a document collator that would attach to the Xerox copier, including a cost versus savings estimate. But senior management rejected the proposal. That was disappointing because if it had been accepted, not only would it have made our work more efficient, but I would have received a bonus equal to ten percent of the first year's savings.

&

I do not know how it happened, but my boss found out that I had transitioned. He was not happy about that. But at about the same time, a few days before Thanksgiving, a US Army Lieutenant Colonel came into my office and asked permission to post some Army Reserve Recruiting Posters in the employee's lounge. I granted permission and walked him down to the lounge. As I assisted in putting up a couple of posters, he asked if I would be interested in joining.

I said, "Yes, but I'm not eligible."

He asked me how old I was. When I told him that I was 35, he replied, "That's too old unless you have prior service."

I told him I had been a Chief Petty Officer in the US Navy and Naval Reserve with 12 years of active and four-years of reserve service.

He responded, "Then, you are eligible."

I said, "No, I'm not. The Navy discharged me because I was undergoing sex reassignment from male to female."

The Colonel responded, "Wow, did you see *Medical Center* with Robert Reed, last night? That was an amazing program."[61]

I said, "Yes, I did. I consulted on it."

He followed with, "I don't understand why you can't come back to the military. It's obvious you can still do your job."

I said, "Of course, I can."

He then asked, "Let me look into it. Please, send me your DD-214Ns."

After some thought, I sent my DD-214Ns to the Lieutenant Colonel at the 49th Medical Battalion. A week or so later, I received a call from him telling me that if I could pass the physical, I could join as a Sergeant First Class (E7), which was equivalent to my Chief Petty Officer rating in the Navy/Naval Reserve. The next day, I drove to the Joint Forces

---

[61] Released September 15, 1975, actor Robert Reed played a doctor who undergoes a sex change operation. The two-part episode was called *The Fourth Sex*, it earned Reed an Emmy nomination, https://www.imdb.com/title/tt0063928/, https://www.youtube.com/watch?v=Z4JHvizrxr4&feature=youtu.be, https://laughingsquid.com/brady-bunch-actor-robert-reed-played-a-transgendered-doctor-1975/.

Training Base, Los Alamitos, and I filled out all of the paperwork, taking care to ensure that all my responses were

accurate. For example, "Have you ever been known by another name?" The next weekend, I underwent a full physical examination and passed. Finally, on 6 February 1976, I was sworn in as a Sergeant First Class and assigned to the 49th Medical Battalion as its Personnel Staff NCO.

Figure 13: Joanna Clark, US Army

Over the next two weekend drill periods, I began to make friends with my new military comrades.

At about this time, Jude introduced me to Christine Jorgensen. It turned out we were practically neighbors, as she lived slightly less than two miles from my parents. The day we met, I was in uniform. The Army thought I'd look good on a recruiting poster, and I had just returned from a photoshoot. Jude introduced me.

Chris asked, "Do they know?" I told her a few at the command level were aware. Chris replied, "Your time will come."

In late April, we went to Fort Ord[62] for our annual two-week training exercise. Being a medical battalion, the focus of our training was delivering emergency medicine. I had certification as a CPR instructor, so I re-certified everyone.

Later, near the end of our training deployment, I discovered that I had been ineligible for reenlistment. Army Medical Regulation 40-501, paragraph 2.13s explicitly stated that I was ineligible for appointment, enlistment, or induction into the service. However, Chapter 3, which dealt with pre-existing conditions, made no mention of the condition outlined in Chapter 2, paragraph 2-13s. I had been enlisted for more than 120 days, so Chapter 2 no longer applied. My pre-existing condition had not prevented me from performing my duties or responsibilities, so Chapter 3 was applicable, and it made no mention of sex reassignment.

I went to the Lieutenant Colonel and showed him the regulation. He went in and talked to the Commanding Officer, then came out and said, "Don't worry about it." This was long before "Don't ask. Don't tell."[63]

---

[62] Fort Ord is a former United States Army post on Monterey Bay of the Pacific coast in California, which closed in 1994 due to Base Realignment and Closure (BRAC) action. Most of the fort's land now makes up the Fort Ord National Monument, managed by the United States Bureau of Land Management as part of the National Conservation Lands, while a small portion remains an active military installation under Army control designated as the Ord Military Community. See https://en.m.wikipedia.org/wiki/Fort_Ord.

[63] Former official US policy (1993–2011, coined after President Bill Clinton signed into law a directive that military personnel "don't ask, don't tell, don't pursue, and don't harass," theoretically lifted a ban on homosexual service in the military that had been instituted during World War II, https://www.britannica.com/event/Dont-Ask-Dont-Tell.

Everything was fine until they put me in for promotion to Warrant Officer and then all hell broke loose. It all began on the trip home. The Command Sergeant Major asked if I would be interested in coming on board full-time as an Army Reserve Technician.[64]

I said, "Yes."

The next day, I applied, and a week later, I was hired. I served notice at the County of Orange, and two weeks later, I left my County job for an Army Reserve Technician (GS5) position with the 63rd Army Command (ARCOM).

A month later, I interviewed for a GS7 position with the Commanding Officer of the 306th Psychological Operations[65] Battalion, Fort MacArthur, [66] San Pedro, California. The

---

[64] A military technician (dual status) is a Federal civilian employee who is:

> a) employed under section 3101 of title 5 or section 709(b) of title 32;
> b) required as a condition of that employment to maintain membership in the Selected Reserve; and
> c) assigned to a civilian position as a technician in the organizing, administering, instructing, or training of the Selected Reserve or in the maintenance and repair of supplies or equipment issued to the Selected Reserve or the armed forces.

[65] Psychological Operations Specialists are influence experts, who assesses the information needs of a target population and craft messaging to influence and engage target audiences. See https://www.goarmy.com/careers-and-jobs/browse-career-and-job-categories/intelligence-and-combat-support/psychological-operations-specialist.html.

[66] Fort MacArthur is a former United States Army installation in San Pedro, Los Angeles, California (now the port community of Los Angeles). A small section remains in military use by the United States

Commanding Officer hired me at the end of the interview, and a week later, I transferred from the 63rd ARCOM to the 306th Psychological Operations Battalion.

&

One afternoon, I had to take care of some business in Santa Ana, and I decided to stop in and say hello to my former staff. I was surprised to see that a collator had been installed on the Xerox copier.

I asked when they got the collator, and they said about a week or two after I left. I went down to Personnel to see what had happened. The clerk pulled up the suggestion and found that it had been submitted by my former supervisor the day after my departure. The supervisor had changed the date on my submission and signed his name, pocketing my reward for himself.

The clerk pulled my submission from the archive and took it over to the Board of Supervisors. Two weeks later, I received an apology and a check. My former supervisor got a reprimand and had to return the money he had received.

&

I now began to settle in at the 306th. What I found was an administrative disaster. The Senior Staff Administrator (SSA) was a Warrant Officer. The other three were all lower-ranked

---

Air Force as a housing and administrative annex of Los Angeles Air Force Base. The fort is named after Lieutenant General Arthur MacArthur. His son, Douglas MacArthur, would later command American forces in the Pacific during World War II.

enlisted staff. I was assigned to the S2 (Intelligence), supporting Major Michael Aquino, the Battalion Intelligence Officer.

The SSA assigned a small office space that isolated me from the other staff. I had the feeling that this was because I outranked all but the SSA. The best thing about the office assignment was that it was secure. I found a desk, file cabinet, and a couple of bookcases and moved them into my new office.

The SSA gave me a box of applications to review. Some of them were over a year old. I felt that I needed to talk to the applicants, but I couldn't find an alert roster. I asked the SSA for a copy, but it was out of date.

The next six-months passed quickly. I replaced all of the outdated military regulations in the Regulations Library, created a new alert roster for the Battalion, and scheduled all language school applicants to attend Monterey. In December 1976, the Battalion received an award for most improvement.

In my off-duty time, I worked with Jude, lecturing to human sexuality students at our local community colleges and universities. The Erickson Educational Foundation, a transsexual education organization, had been taken over by Dr. Paul Walker and renamed the Janus Information Facility.

I had helped rewrite the Erickson educational pamphlet "Legal Aspects of Transsexualism," and Paul asked me to update it again.[67]

I began writing letters to Social Security, the State Department, and the Rehabilitation Services Administration (RSA) seeking policy changes. Social Security ultimately agreed to update their records upon presentation of a legal name change and a certified letter that sex reassignment surgery (SRS) had been completed.

Legal Aspects of Transsexualism

1990 Edition

Sr Mary Elizabeth, SSE

Figure 14: Cover of **Legal Aspects of Transsexualism**

The State Department recognized the problem a passport could create for individuals going overseas for SRS. They agreed that upon the presentation of a legal name change and letter from the individual's physician stating the trip's purpose was to undergo SRS, a one-year temporary passport would be issued with a corrected name and gender.

૨ઍ

---

[67] Mary Elizabeth Clark, International Foundation for Gender Education, 1979, ISBN 978-0962597602, see http://lvtgw.jadephoenix.org/Info_htm/TgLaw/tg_law02.htm.

In the meantime, the SSA was medically retired following an automobile accident, resulting in my promotion to Acting SSA.

There was a glitch with this promotion, however. The position required I be at least a Warrant Officer. The command submitted nomination papers calling for my promotion to Warrant Officer. In the next two weeks, the gates to hell on earth swung open.

I called Christine Jorgensen and asked her if she remembered what she had said when we first met.

She replied, "Yes. I said, 'Your time will come'."

I replied, "Well, it has come."

Chris suggested I come over, and we set a time. She also invited Shearlean Duke, a friend and investigative reporter with the Los Angeles Times. I brought a copy of the Alert Roster with me.

I brought Christine and Shearlean up to date on what had happened so far. A Judge Advocate General (JAG) officer from the 351st Civil Affairs Command was interviewing staff, and the investigation was ongoing.

Shearlean agreed she would not publish anything until a final determination was reached. She would, however, begin an investigation of her own.

I told her, "No problem," and handed her a copy of the Alert Roster.

Shearlean started interviewing members of the Battalion, beginning with the lowest-ranking members. By the time she reached the Executive Officer (XO), she had her story. The

XO hung up on her, and a "no comment" order was issued. The order was too late though. Shearlean already had her story.[68]

The next two months were a nightmare. Finally, the Army sent me to the Long Beach Naval Hospital for a physical examination. A Navy physician, Captain Jose Smith, was assigned to give me a physical. Midway through my medical examination, he stopped.

"This is too important. Can you come back tomorrow morning?" he asked.

I looked at him, confused.

"I want you examined by the head of each department. They are all Navy Captains, board-certified in their specialty," he said.

The next morning, I checked in at 0800. Captain Smith told me not to tell them that I had been through sex reassignment unless they specifically asked. Over the next six hours, I was examined by a psychiatrist, OB-GYN, internal medicine/endocrinologist, and an orthopedist. Only the OB-GYN questioned why he had been told to perform an examination that any Lieutenant Junior Grade (LTJG) could perform. I told him.

He responded, "Now I can say that I've seen everything, but I still don't understand. There's nothing wrong with you that I can see. Do you have any complaints?"

I said, "No!"

---

[68] See Duke, "Transsexual Wars with the Army," Los Angeles Times (Sept 14, 1977).

The next morning, I met with the team. They found me "Disqualified based on the current wording of AR 40-501, para. 2.13s. Qualified physically and psychologically to perform the duties of her rank and position."

The following morning the Army voided my enlistment.

On 14 September 1977, Shearlean ran her story "Transsexual Wars with the Army" in the Los Angeles Times, and within hours, I was receiving calls for interviews and appearances on the television talk show circuit. I also received a call from an attorney, offering to represent me *pro bono*.

We filed our case against the Department of the Army in December 1977, seeking reinstatement.

For the next couple of months, I did the television talk show circuit: *Good Morning America, the Phil Donahue Show, Sally Jesse Raphael, Larry King, Tom Snyder*, plus several local talk shows, along with meeting regularly with my new attorney.

All the publicity I was getting made it impossible to get a job. I returned to college on the GI Bill and started a secretarial service. Over the next three years, I earned an Associate in Arts degree in Human Services and an Associate in Science degree in Electronics Technology, and a Bachelor of Arts degree in Liberal Studies, with minors in Psychology and Sociology, from the State University of New York at Albany.

The ACLU Years—1980-1986

My lawsuit against the Secretary of the Army was moving slowly forward. The case was eventually settled out of court in 1982. I received an Honorable Discharge, credit for time served, and a monetary settlement, with a stipulation that details of the settlement not be made public. In the end, I am the first person to serve in two branches of the US military in two different genders. I also completed my college studies by the end of the decade and received my degrees.

After that, I successfully advocated for replacement birth certificates and driver's licenses for transgender people in California. In 1980, I helped co-found the ACLU Transsexual Rights Committee, which I chaired for many years. Among other things, the ACLU Transsexual Rights Committee advocated for government and private insurance coverage for sex reassignment surgery.

In my spare time, I lectured with Jude at our local colleges and continued working on "community issues." In November 1977, Jude had heard that the infamous John R. Brown[69] was getting involved with a support group in Laguna Beach, run by William Heard, a Clinical Psychologist.

Jude went alone to visit Dr. Heard at one of the group meetings and found that one of the group members was engaged in attempting to lure some of the trans women to

---

[69] See https://en.wikipedia.org/wiki/John_Ronald_Brown, https://murderpedia.org/male.B/b/brown-john-ronald.htm.

have Dr. Brown do their surgery in exchange for Dr. Brown doing her surgery for free. Dr. Heard did not know about Dr. Brown's terrible reputation and, after talking with Jude, he warned his clients about Dr. Brown.

Figure 15: Secretary Elaine, Joanna, Jude Patton, Dr. Heard
Gender Dysphoria Group of Orange County

Jude invited me to join him in visiting the group during its December meeting. We exposed Brown again, and a nearly two-decade relationship began with Dr. Heard, with the formation of the Gender Dysphoria Program of Orange County.

At about the same time, Paul Walker, a Clinical Psychologist, who headed up the Janus Information Facility, had developed AIDS, and he asked Jude and I to take over Janus. But there was one catch, we couldn't use the Janus name. Jude and I accepted Paul's request and renamed it the J2CP (J2=Joanna + Jude, CP=Clark + Patton) Information Service.

I worked through various temporary employment agencies from October 1977 to December 1979. Then, in January 1980, I was invited to come to work with the ACLU of Southern California.

In February 1980, I asked Ramona Ripston, the Executive Director, and Fred Okrand, the Legal Director, to create the first ACLU Transsexual Rights Committee, comprising a small group of trans activists. They approved my request and assigned Susan McGreivy, their gay rights attorney, to advise us.

Unable to find affordable housing in the local area, the 120-mile daily round trip took its toll on me. In late-March 1980, I resigned, returned to my parents' home in San Juan Capistrano, and reestablished my secretarial service.

The ACLU had several Orange County attorneys assisting in local cases, so they hired me to provide clerical support. On two occasions, I took my word processor to the ACLU offices in Los Angeles, when cases to which I had been providing clerical support went to trial.

In the meantime, the ACLU Transsexual Rights Committee received a request for assistance from a "jailhouse lawyer." [70] This particular jailhouse lawyer was seeking assistance for a preoperative male-to-female (MtF) inmate who was being abused by the Federal Bureau of Prisons (FBoP) staff.

I drove down to San Diego to the Federal Holding Facility to see her, but the staff refused me access. I was allowed to speak with her jailhouse lawyer, however.

The jailhouse lawyer explained the prisoner's history leading to her incarceration. She had attempted suicide but was found unconscious, and she was treated in an Emergency Room (ER) in Tacoma, Washington. The ER staff, discovering that she was a "he," released her instead of placing her on a 72-hour psychiatric hold.

Still suicidal, she robbed a bank the next day, hoping that the police would kill her when she pointed a gun at them. After nearly 20 minutes, without the police arriving, she left the bank and walked down the street to a second bank, which she robbed and, again, waited for the police. She watched as the police went to the first bank. Frustrated, she left and walked to her car, where she drove from Tacoma to Atlanta, Georgia. During the drive, she worked through her depression and suicidal thoughts and decided to enroll in an introductory class in psychology, hoping to learn why she felt the way she did about her gender.

In trouble with the law himself, her brother obtained Annie's location from his mother under the pretense of reconnecting with her. He told the authorities where they would find Annie in exchange for a lighter sentence.

---

[70] A jailhouse lawyer is a prison inmate who, despite no legal education, studies law and argues for the rights of other inmates.

Ironically, the FBI only had circumstantial evidence. None of the bank employees could identify her, and none of the bank cameras had obtained a picture of her. But Annie would not lie. She confessed, explaining why she robbed the banks.

The judge called her "a menace to society." He then sentenced Annie to serve 15 years on each count, to be served concurrently. The judge also said she would serve her time in an all-male prison, which resulted in another suicide attempt.

If Annie had not been a transsexual, she might not have been treated as a menace to society. It is highly likely that she would have been sent to a mental facility for evaluation and treatment, the treatment that might have included sex-reassignment surgery given the numerous legal decisions of the 1970s and early 1980s.[71] All of these cases concluded that sex-reassignment was a medically necessary treatment procedure when treating a transsexual.

As a result of the suicide attempt, Annie was evaluated by a local psychiatrist from the University of Washington, then sent to the Federal Bureau of Prisons Medical Facility at Springfield for medical and psychiatric evaluation. Medical staff suggested that she might be Intersex, but no assessment was performed. It was written in her record that she should not be housed or transported with males.

However, the FBoP, in its infinite wisdom, ordered her sent to the Federal Correctional Institution (FCI) Pleasanton, where she was housed with males, immediately raped, and placed in Administrative Segregation (AdSeg) for 30 days.

It was here that Sara Jane Moore entered the picture. Sara, serving a life sentence for the attempted assassination of US

---

[71] See G.B. vs Lackner, J.D. vs Lackner, Rush vs Parham, etc.

President Gerald Ford in 1975, was transferred to FCI Pleasanton, and placed in AdSeg, in a cell adjacent to Annie. Sara assessed that Annie was suicidal, and she convinced Annie that prison authorities wanted her to commit suicide. She taught Annie how to fight them, which led Annie to experience a grand tour of the FBoP system.

When Annie's 30 days in AdSeg were up, she refused to leave. Consequently, the staff arranged to transfer Annie to another facility. She was moved temporarily to the Metropolitan Correctional Center (MCC) San Diego, where the ACLU of Southern California's Transsexual Rights Committee and I became involved with her case.

I called Ramona Ripston the next morning, and she arranged for an ACLU volunteer attorney to visit Annie that afternoon. Within minutes of the visit, the FBoP transferred Annie to FCI Butner, North Carolina.

Annie had my name and toll-free telephone number, and upon release from AdSeg at FCI Butner, she called and left a message as to where she was. I notified Ramona, and she contacted the ACLU of North Carolina. They, in turn, sent an attorney to interview Annie.

Within minutes of the visiting attorney's departure, Annie was on the move again. It would take nearly two months for Annie to surface. When she did, she was back in FCI Pleasanton.

ॐ

During this time, Diane Saunders, one of the most knowledgeable paralegals I have ever met, had joined ACLU Attorney Susan McGreivy and me on Annie's case. Diane argued that we would have better luck if we dropped all of the defendants except the Federal Bureau of Prisons Director. His office was in the District of Columbia: consequently, if we filed in the District of Columbia, where the defendant resided, it would not matter which prison they sent Annie to. Diane prepared the documents, and we got them to Annie when she resurfaced. We got the new documents to Annie. She signed the papers, and Susan forwarded them to the ACLU office in Washington, DC, for filing in the US District Court for the District of Columbia. The DC judge assigned to hear the case transferred it to San Francisco, where we drew Judge Conti, better known as the "Hanging Judge."

At this point, a new attorney, fresh out of law school and newly admitted to the Bar, joined the team. Amanda had shown up at my office to tell me to stop practicing law without a license. I informed her that technically I wasn't, nor was Diane, as Susan was supervising us. As a team, we were assisting Annie, who was filing In Pro Per.[72]

The Director then petitioned the court to transfer Annie to the State of California facility at Vacaville. Vacaville is where California housed the most dangerous criminals, like Charles Manson, the quasi-commune leader who committed nine murders in July and August 1969. Judge Conti approved the custody transfer.

Just out of law school, our new attorney joined me on our first visit to Vacaville to meet her first client. We went over the documents that we had brought with us. Annie signed the letter appointing Amanda as her attorney and initialed the

---

[72] A term derived from the Latin "in propria persona," meaning "for one's self," used in some states to describe a person who handles his or her case, without a lawyer.

Temporary Restraining Order (TRO). Then, we headed over to Sacramento to the Federal Court to file the documents.

As we departed the court clerk's office, we ran into a reporter with the Sacramento Bee. He asked what we were doing, and Amanda and I discussed Annie's case with him. He asked if he could go out and interview her, and we said, "Yes." The next morning the reporter went out to Vacaville and interviewed Annie. He also took pictures of her. He then called me to inform me that I was famous. He had recognized me during our meeting at the courthouse.

I said, "Apparently, but I'm not the story."

He promised not to mention me, and he kept his word. The story ran on the front page of the Sacramento Bee the next morning.

I cannot help but believe that Judge Ramirez, who drew Annie's case, read the article while eating breakfast. Amanda presented our evidence, and the US Attorney argued the government's position. When finished, without batting an eye, Judge Ramirez granted our TRO, set a date for the Preliminary Injunction hearing, and ordered Annie transferred to FBoP Terminal Island to be closer to us. To say that the US Attorney was stunned would have been an understatement.

Annie's mental health began to deteriorate during this period. Vacaville was a real hellhole, and Annie lived in constant fear. She had never experienced love in her family. Her parents and siblings, except for her younger sister, Julie, had rejected her, treating her at times quite brutally. This treatment eventually resulted in Child Services removing her for her safety.

While Annie's physical safety improved, neither Child Services nor the family providing her lodging had the training to provide the mental health support she desperately needed. Consequently, she eventually ran away to live on the streets, which led to her attempted suicide in Tacoma, Washington.

Because of this, I decided to adopt her, and for a while, her spirits improved. Amanda drew up the adoption papers, and Orange County Superior Court Judge James Judge approved the adoption on January 11, 1983, wishing her "all the happiness in the world." The judge vacated his order the next day after learning we were transsexuals.

Jude and I set out to find some experts to evaluate Annie. We found three: Professor Richard Green, M.D. (Psychiatrist), author of *Transsexualism and Sex Reassignment*; Paul Walker, Ph.D. (Clinical Psychologist), JANUS Information Facility; and Dr. Smith [73] at the University of Washington. Dr. Smith had performed a psychiatric evaluation following Annie's attempted suicide in her cell after being told she would be going to a male prison, and he was able to provide a baseline.

The FBoP provided a single expert. She held a Master's degree in Sociology and had co-authored a chapter in a Human Sexuality textbook. She had never seen Annie.

At the end of the arguments, Judge Ramirez broke for 30 minutes, then returned with his decision.

He began with, "If it looks like a duck, and sounds like a duck, it is most likely a duck." After a short pause, he continued, "Ms. Mostyn looks like a young woman, she

---

[73] A pseudonym.

sounds and has the mannerisms of a young woman, and she is most likely a woman."

Then, he ordered her sent to FBoP Lexington, housed in a single cell with the women, treated as a woman, and allowed to gain an education and a job.

Judge Rameriz closed with a line from *The Godfather*, addressed to the US attorney, telling him that if he received any reports that his order was being violated, he would hold the FBoP in contempt of court.

Annie was paroled two years later. She visited me a couple of times. On her last visit, Annie informed me that she was relocating to Hawaii. She had certified as a phlebotomist, and she hoped to become a registered nurse (RN) and a SCUBA instructor.

I was a Professional Association of Diving Instructors Master SCUBA Instructor, but my failing health had forced me to give up diving. So, I took Annie out to my storage locker and gave her my equipment. It was the last time I saw her as she relocated to Honolulu, Hawaii, the following week.

In Honolulu, she obtained work at The Queen's Medical Center. When not working, she attended school, training to become a Registered Nurse, and she also qualified as a SCUBA Instructor.

She continued working at The Queen's Medical Center. Occasionally, she would get floated to the upper floors where patients were being admitted. It was here that tragedy struck. She suffered a needlestick while drawing blood on a patient. The lab had failed to provide proper equipment, and the lack of appropriate equipment led to Annie receiving approximately 1 cc of drawn blood in her thumb. Annie followed proper protocol and had her blood tested for HIV. The patient died from end-stage AIDS before her results came back.

Annie obtained an attorney and sued the lab for its failure to provide appropriate safety equipment. The case went on for several years, eventually settling in her favor.

Figure 16: Joanna teaching SCUBA

Following the settlement, Annie relocated to Oregon, where she purchased a home with land that allowed her to have a horse and some goats. She lived with and suffered from HIV/AIDS for 11 years. Her love for her animals and friends gave her the strength to persevere. AIDS finally took her life in 2003.

ॐ

I had settled my case with the Department of the Army in 1982. In 1986, I assisted the ACLU in upgrading to modern word processors, which ultimately reduced my involvement. A new chapter in my journey was about to begin.

Finding a Cause

As my time with ACLU projects began to slow down, I began to rebuild my secretarial service. Two events would set me on a new path, however. The first was gallbladder sickness, lasting nine months, and the second was the rebirth of feelings about a religious life.

If I had had Blue Cross or Blue Shield health insurance, my gallbladder problems would most likely have lasted no more than a month or two because the Mission Hospital ER was only 10 minutes from my home. Unfortunately, at the time, I had Kaiser Permanente, an HMO plan, and, at the time, the closest Kaiser ER was at Lakeview and I-91, about 32 miles distant. Drive time to the ER averaged 45 minutes and wait times to be seen by a physician averaged 50 to 90 minutes. Consequently, by the time a physician saw me, the attack was winding down, and my status was no longer an emergency. Over nine months, I averaged two visits per week to the ER. Finally, my condition deteriorated to justify gallbladder surgery, and the ER physician referred me for surgery.

I arrived for my appointment at the surgery clinic at the scheduled time. A nurse came in and drew blood, and after a short wait, the surgeon entered the room. He began to ask me the routine panel of questions, and I added to his list of surgeries I had experienced by telling him that I had been through sex reassignment.

I always make it a point to tell the surgeon because they don't remove the prostate during MtF sex reassignment surgery, and I didn't want it mistaken for cancer.

The surgeon wrote "sex change" on my surgical history form: then, without a word, he left the examination room and didn't return. I finally dressed and left the room, where I caught a nurse leaving the office. She had a surprised look on her face when she saw me. She asked what I was doing there.

I told her, "I was being seen by the surgeon when he walked out of the room without saying a word, and he didn't come back."

She told me he had left for the day, and she was closing up. She made another appointment for me, but it was three days later.

I had another attack on day two, and my neighbor drove me to the ER. This time, they had to come out to the car and get me. The nurse drew blood, and the doctor came in to check on me.

He said, "Surgery, NOW!" and they took me straight to surgery.

The surgeon—not the one I had seen before—arrived. I regained consciousness about five or six hours later in a room on the pediatrics floor. Plastic bags filled with what looked like waste lined the wall.

I could see nurses moving up and down the hallway outside my doorway, but they ignored my cries for assistance. Finally, one came in, but she wasn't very forthcoming with answers to my questions. Later, a nurse came in and took my vital signs, but she left without a word.

Later in the day, I had an unexpected visitor, one of the ACLU attorneys I assisted periodically visited me. He had tried to reach me, and my parents told him I had had emergency surgery the night before. If he had not visited me when he did, I'm not sure I would have survived the ordeal. He wasted no time complaining about how I was being treated.

My friend, Jude Patton, a trans man who is an LMFT and Physician Assistant, also visited me soon after I called him to let him know how poorly I was being treated. He told me later that when he arrived on my hospital floor, he found me in what looked like an unkempt storage room, in a pediatric-sized hospital bed. I had been left unattended, uncomfortable, and obviously in pain, with my feet extended past the end of the small bed (I am 6 feet one inch tall).

He found that my name was missing on the nurses' call board. He overheard nurses using incorrect pronouns to address me and witnessed their derisive behaviors toward me. Seeing them ignore my pleas for aid, Jude immediately marched up to the nurses' station and demanded to talk to the nursing supervisor about my neglectful care. After several false starts, a supervisor finally arrived.

Using his professional titles and status as a healthcare practitioner, Jude instantly became my advocate, telling her in no uncertain terms that I needed to be treated appropriately and with dignity and respect. Then, he got them to bring in an adult-sized hospital bed and got me safely transferred. He also got them to write my name and pertinent care information on the nurses' call board. He spent a good deal of time attempting to educate the nurse supervisor and other hospital staff about transgender issues and demanded that my care be given over to more understanding and compassionate nursing staff. He also let them know that he would be checking on me daily and would initiate complaints about staff who were mistreating me.

After my hospitalization, I filed complaints to the hospital Board of Directors and the state medical board. My complaints were ignored and essentially denied. However, Jude filed written complaints separately and received a letter of apology, a veiled admission of wrongdoing. Jude gave me his letter to use as I pleased if I decided to file a medical malpractice lawsuit.

The entire experience was an eye-opener for me, as I had never experienced or even imagined that this degree of discrimination could be directed towards a fellow human being.

However, the complaints and the hiring of a new Chief Executive Medical Officer (CEMO), brought about significant changes, all positive. It began with the publication of a handbook detailing how the staff was to respond with respect and professionalism to LGBTQ patients.

ॐ

The second event revolved around my attitude towards organized religion. If you recall from an earlier chapter, I was an active member of the Baptist Church when I entered the Navy. I was active to the point of planning to enroll in the Moody Bible Institute in Chicago at the end of my Naval service.

I attended my first Mass in 1945 when we lived across the street from St. Michael's Catholic Church. My parents had allowed me to attend Mass with the Donahue family, who lived a house away from us on Lewis Street. I came home from Mass one Sunday in 1946 and announced to my parents that I was going to be a sister when I grew up. That was the last Mass I would attend until 1987, 41 years later. The next Sunday, I was sitting in a pew at our local First Baptist Church.

But I was an outsider in the Baptist Church. I never felt like I belonged there. We lived in a Catholic neighborhood, and, except for one, my friends were all Catholic. After a couple of months, I told my parents I didn't feel welcome with the Baptists, and I stopped attending church for the next decade.

The racial bias I was exposed to while stationed in Norman, Oklahoma, and Memphis, Tennessee, bothered me to a large extent. I had become a Christian during my second year of high school, and racism did not seem to fit within Christ's teaching. In Matthew 22:37-40, particularly Matthew 22:39, Jesus said, "Love your neighbor as yourself." He did *not* say, "Love your neighbor as yourself, *except for* people of color or people you perceive as different."

Upon completion of my training in Memphis, I was assigned to Patrol Squadron 49, NOB Bermuda. Bermuda was as confusing to me as the southern United States had been. I became a member of the Portuguese Baptist Church during my first month in Bermuda only to learn that, on the island, the Portuguese were considered to be second-class citizens. Interracial marriage between Whites and people of color was readily accepted, however. I struggled with this throughout my time in Bermuda. It was not until I returned to

Memphis for a tour of instructor duty that my religious views underwent a dramatic change.

It began on a Sunday morning when I invited a sailor friend and his wife to attend church. We had often attended church together in Bermuda, and they arrived in Memphis about six months after I did.

My friend was African American, and his wife was African-Bermudian. Whenever they met someone for the first time, they automatically assumed that the wife was White, and their marriage was interracial. She was, however, of Black descent. She just looked white.

Interracial marriage did not become legal in the United States until 1967, following the US Supreme Court decision *Loving v. Virginia. Loving v. Virginia* ruled that race-based restrictions on marriages, such as the anti-miscegenation law in Virginia, violated the Equal Protection Clause of the United States Constitution.

On our first Sunday together, I invited my friend and his wife to join me at church. But my African American friend was not welcome. Initially, his wife was, as the pastor assumed that she was my wife. When he learned that she was married to a person of color, she was no longer welcome either. I could not accept this kind of hatred within a church supposedly based on love: consequently, I left and did not set foot in a church for two decades.

Then, one morning in 1987, I came across a newspaper article about a local Episcopal priest. The people in the neighborhood, where the church—St. Clements Episcopal Church—was located, wanted him removed. His sin? Christian love for the less fortunate. He was leaving the church open at night to provide the homeless with a place of safety.

Following my return from Vietnam, I had learned that any number of causative factors could lead to homelessness: for example, lack of affordable housing, unemployment, poor physical or mental health, drug and alcohol abuse, family and relationship breakdown, domestic violence, physical or sexual abuse. Any one of these could lead to a person becoming homeless.

It had been 41 years since I attended Catholic Mass and 26 years since I walked away from religion in Memphis. This time, I attended an Episcopal Mass, and I felt like I was home.

The AIDS pandemic had become global, and Orange County had its share of victims. One of the women I met at St. Clements was Julia Rae Walz. Julia Rae was on the Diocese Council, and she went off to Chicago for a national meeting. I had been with the church for about two months when she returned. At the morning Mass, Father Bob asked her about the conference and did she have anything planned.

She said, Yes, we are going to start an AIDS Support Group."

You could have heard a pin drop. Father Bob asked for comments, and the response was, "When do we start?" I volunteered.

While attending class to be received into the Episcopal Church, I mentioned my interest in the sisterhood. They told me there was a community in San Francisco, and I contacted them. The following month, after being received into the church, I drove to San Francisco and spent two weeks with the Community of St. Francis.

Three weeks later, after spending time with Father Bob and a spiritual director from the Diocese, I asked to return. I drove back to San Francisco and asked to join as a Novice. The Community was small, and they had valid concerns about how the Diocese membership would respond to my presence, especially since the press was still interested in me because of my lawsuit against the Department of the Army, and because of the increased public awareness and interest in my having undergone sex reassignment. The Mother Superior suggested that I apply to the Third Order community. I told her I had, and they had suggested that I belonged in a First Order community, such as the Community of St. Francis.

The Mother Superior looked at the clock and said, "It's time for noon prayer."

We joined the rest of the Community in the Chapel. After prayers, we adjourned to the dining room for lunch. After lunch, I went to my room, followed by Mother Superior. We sat down, and she gave me the Community's decision. I packed my bag, loaded it in my car, then went in, and thanked everyone for allowing me to visit. An hour later, I reached the I5-South and headed for home.

A few days later, I met with my spiritual director and Father Bob. My spiritual director told me to write to a Community in the United Kingdom for their instruction manual on how to create a new Community. I wrote them a letter, included a donation to cover publication costs and International postage costs.

The book arrived a month later, and I began to draft the documents, circulating them to my spiritual director and a Monsignor at the Diocese. Father Bob suggested that I make vows on Epiphany, January 6, 1988. I discussed it with my spiritual director, and I sent a note to the Monsignor at the Diocese, letting him know our plans.

A few days later, I received a call from Jean Pasco, a reporter with the Orange County Register. She had learned that I was about to make vows. I told her it was a private matter, and I wanted no press. I immediately called my contacts at the church and told them of the development. I suggested we postpone my making vows until the press lost interest. They said that they would discuss the matter and get back to me.

Figure 17: Sister Mary Elizabeth

A couple of days later, I received a call back. They had decided that if the press showed up, it was because God wanted them there. I tried to explain that they didn't understand. It would not be a three-ring circus: it would be a five-ring nightmare. Still, I made my vows during Epiphany, on January 6, 1988, as planned.

Epiphany arrived, and the Mass began at 6:00 pm. Jean Paseo, representing the Orange County Register, was there to cover the event. Her story went out on the wire the next morning at 2 am, and the circus was underway by 7:30 am. Every local television station had a truck parked in front of the church when I arrived.

I went out on the sidewalk and told them that they were welcome to attend morning Mass, but no cameras would be allowed inside the church. As I recall, we had an above-average attendance at Mass that morning, so not all was lost.

By mid-morning, it was clear that we would get no work done. The phone was constantly ringing, and the courtyard was packed with reporters and camera personnel, trying to get an exclusive. Finally, I slipped out a rear window, cut through neighboring yards, and made it to my car. Twenty minutes later, I turned into our mobile home park's main entrance, did a U-turn, and headed for our City Hall. I parked near the Sheriff's substation, took the footbridge across Trabuco Creek, and made my way to our mobile home park's rear gate. I made it to the house directly behind my parent's home and slipped in through our side door from the rear gate.

Figure 18: Sister Mary Elizabeth holding a picture of Michael

Unfortunately, my parents had invited Chuck Henry, a reporter from KABC-7, into the family room. I knew him from my days in Honolulu, Hawaii. Chuck was one of the nightly news reporters on KGMB-TV there, and we had been "dive buddies" on a couple of SCUBA diving trips. Before I could sit down with the "family," the phone in my room rang. It was the church office calling to inform me that they had signed me up to do the Larry King show on CNN that evening, and they would be calling to arrange limo transportation.

While the bulk of the news coverage was positive, it was clear that the Diocese was not happy. It was September before the Bishop would agree to talk to me, and when we did finally speak, it was clear that the new order would never be recognized. There were two other women joining me in the new order, and they chose to move on.

It was decision time. I decided that I had made my vows to God, not just the church, so I renewed my commitment to spend my days helping others where I could.

&

I had been playing with an electronic bulletin board system (BBS) that I pieced together using some shareware I had come across while attending a COMDEX conference in Las Vegas. A gentleman (Terry Travis), who I met at the conference, introduced me to the shareware and FidoNET— a precursor of the Internet—and he helped me get connected. My address was 1:103/927. Globally, there were some 65,000 BBSs, connected by phone lines. It was fun to toy with, but, at the time, I had no idea what I could do with it.

I began to feel that I was no longer welcome in the Episcopal Church, but I still felt that God had called me for some reason. My vows were to God first, the church second.

I decided that I would concentrate on helping the homeless and children living in the local HUD housing project. On weekdays, I volunteered at the local ESA Homeless Facility in San Clemente. Weekends, I would spend with the children.

We spent weekends exploring the Museums in San Diego's Balboa Park, Griffith and Mount Wilson Observatories, and the California Science Center in Exposition Park, Los Angeles. The group was fascinated by science and history.

I gave the children a project to write a paper on "Why they would like to go to the Moon and Mars." The writer of the "best paper" would get to go to Space Camp in Huntsville, Alabama. The young man whose paper won went to Space Camp for the one-week Astronaut training program. The next month, I made the same offer to the group again. This time, the winner was a young girl, but her mother refused to allow her to attend Space Camp. I had already reserved and paid for the space. None of the other children were available, so I asked our young astronaut if he'd like to go back for the second, advanced class. He said, "Yes," and his mother gave her approval. I called Huntsville and was allowed to upgrade the reservation to the two-week "advanced" course.

A few months later, I received an invitation to attend a meeting in Kansas City. I accepted and, there, I met a young woman who was interested in what I was doing. She owned a small farm outside of Stover, Missouri, where she raised Black Angus cows, and she invited me to join her.

Returning to my parents' home had worked out for the most part. Well, until I made vows. Then, my father went absolutely ballistic. If you were looking for somebody who followed the teaching of Christ, my father walked in his footprints. But he wanted nothing to do with organized religion. His feeling was that if you believe in God, it is a spiritual relationship between you and God. You do not need a bunch of people telling you how to live. In the end, my relationship with my father led me to make a hasty decision. With my dad being so angry over my having made vows, I felt the only solution was to move out. Consequently, by the end of the conference, I had decided to go to Stover to herd the cows that had been donated to the order. A month later, I drove east onto the I-40, and three days later, I pulled into the driveway at the farm.

Figure 19: Sister Mary Elizabeth with Jude Patton's mom

Stover was an interesting place. The population was 1,013, and there were no jobs. I was an outsider and being an Episcopal sister did not mitigate that at all. In fact, in some respects, it complicated things. There was a Catholic church in Stover, but it was locked up during the week. On Sunday morning, the cars pulled in, the priest arrived, held a mass, and out the door he would go. Then, the church was locked, and everybody went home. And that was it for another week. A circuit-riding priest, he had six parishes to cover.

Their doctor was also a circuit rider, who came to town every Wednesday afternoon for four hours. Everyone had party-lines. Private telephone lines were limited to the few businesses in town. The next town east of Stover was Versailles, with about 2,475 residents and a Walmart.

On my second or third trip to the Walmart store in Versailles, I met a young man in the parking lot. It looked like he needed some help, so I walked over to him. It was then that I noticed the lesion on his face. He was HIV positive. He told me to stay back, that he was sick.

I said, "Yes, you're HIV positive. I recognize the lesion. It's Kaposi sarcoma." [74]

I will never forget the look of terror that came over his face.

He asked, "OMG! How did you know? I've never met you before."

I responded that I had just moved to Stover from Los Angeles and that I had worked with some HIV positive friends. I recognized the Kaposi lesion. He asked me if I

---

[74] A cancer usually appearing as tumors on the skin or mucosal surfaces, the most common type in the United States is AIDS-associated, developing in people who are infected with HIV, the virus that causes AIDS, https://www.cancer.org/cancer/kaposi-sarcoma/about/what-is-kaposi-sarcoma.html.

thought anyone local might recognize it, and I told him I was doubtful.

His fear was fully justified. With everyone having party-lines, he did not dare mention that he was HIV-positive on the telephone. In a small community, with a small post office with only three clerks, it didn't take a brain surgeon to figure out that Box 6003, Rockville, MD 20850, was the National AIDS Information Clearinghouse. All over the country, People with AIDS (PWA) were experiencing having their homes burned to the ground, often with them inside.

I met one other PWA during my stay in Stover. I told them where I lived and said that they were welcome to visit if they ever felt the need to talk, but I never saw them again.

During this time, I received a couple of letters from neighbors back home. They were concerned about my parents, who were both blind, the result of age-related macular degeneration going "wet." They needed me, the neighbors wrote, and my father had finally realized they needed my help. They were asking me to come home.

The situation at the farm wasn't working out all that well either. Linda had failed to mention that she suffered from Post-Traumatic Stress-Disorder (PTSD), and I was spending a great deal of time driving her to the VA Medical Center in Columbia, 80 miles away. I would have to manage the farm during her hospitalizations, something I was ill-equipped to do, having never lived or worked on a farm.

If I returned to California, I would virtually have a full-time job caring for my parents. I'd have a place to live, but they spent the bulk of their time listening to the soap operas on TV. Suddenly, the lightbulb in my head turned on. I could create an online HIV/AIDS information resource using an

Figure 20: Sister Mary Elizabeth

electronic bulletin board system (BBS). If someone picked-up their phone on a party-line, they would hear the beep-beep of the modems talking to each other. The worst-case scenario would be them breaking the connection. And, with FidoNET, I could share the information globally with the geographically isolated.

So, a week later, I packed up the car, signed the cattle back over to the original owner, and headed back to California to look after my parents. Terry Travis put me in touch with Phil Becker, owner of eSoft, who had one of the best BBS software programs—TBBS, with a digital database program called TDBS. Far too expensive for my budget, Phil listened to what I wanted to do, and he agreed to donate the software. Terry flew out from Denver and helped me create the BBS and digital database and updated my registration with FidoNET. I launched the HIV/AIDS Info BBS in November

1989 with a single phone line. The cooling fan noise was a bit much, so I located the BBS in my bathroom, not the most convenient place.

❧

Making vows had another effect. Some people in the transgender community felt uncomfortable with my religious choice and as a result, I withdrew from the community. I will say this, however. I was the happiest person in the world when I came back from surgery and despite all that has happened in my life, I am still very happy. At times, I wish I had transitioned earlier but on the other hand, I have had a lot of experiences that I would not have had otherwise. Overall, I am satisfied. I just wish when the time comes to leave this world, I can leave it a better place than when I arrived.

AIDS and AEGiS

Had it not been for my trip to Stover, Missouri, the seed for AEGiS might never had been planted. A chance meeting with two young men living with AIDS started me on a journey that would captivate my life for the next two and a half decades. I had returned home with a mission. I would create a dedicated, online, HIV/AIDS information resource using an electronic bulletin board system (BBS).

AIDS was considered a "gay" disease in the 1980s, and hatred towards HIV-positive gay persons was beyond comprehension. The young men I met in Stover had every right to be afraid. With everyone having party-lines, they did not dare mention that they were HIV-positive on the telephone.

I am not HIV-positive, but there was another reason I became involved. My treatment following surgery at Kaiser was unprofessional. One of the nurses accused me of being HIV-positive and would not assist me when I needed help. I knew I wasn't HIV-positive because I was neither a drug user sharing needles or sexually active. There was no way I could be HIV-positive unless I had received contaminated blood during my emergency gallbladder surgery the night before. The experience, however, made me realize just how vulnerable PWAs were.

With a single phone line, the TBBS and TDBS software donated by Phil, and an 80-megabyte IBM compatible computer, I began to download AIDS-related information to share, but I quickly ran out of space.

I had subscribed to the National Library of Medicine's "Grateful-MED" to access their AIDSLINE, AIDS DRUGS, and AIDS TRIALS medical databases. I also began writing letters to newspapers and news services worldwide, asking permission to republish their HIV/AIDS news stories and conference abstracts. Access to Grateful-MED was expensive, and I was providing free access to the information. I needed more storage space, more than one phone line, and high-speed modems. That would take money, something I did not have.

Figure 21: Sister Mary Elizabeth working at AEGiS

Toward the end of my first month online, I noticed that government agencies had taken over my BBS phone line. Over the next week, the phone line was inaccessible to non-government callers. People who needed access to the information couldn't access it because government agencies were tying up the line.

I called the National AIDS Policy Office (NAPO) and complained. They suggested that I write to Vice President Al Gore and explain my problem to him. They asked if I had a FAX, and when I said, "Yes," they gave me his FAX number. I thought writing to the Vice President was crazy. What would he do that they couldn't do? But then, what else could I do? It was late on Thursday afternoon when I FAX'd Vice President Al Gore. The next morning at 8 am, I received a phone call from the Office of the Vice-President of the United States. The Vice President had read my letter, and he would handle it. By noon, the number of government agencies online had begun to drop. By Monday, the government agencies had disappeared.

On Monday morning, the National Library of Medicine (NLM) called. They apologized for the problems the various agencies had caused me. They informed me that they had to pay inter-agency fees for accessing Grateful-MED, just like citizens using the service. With that, they gave me a non-billable access code and refunded the previous month's charges. I was about to become an unintended consequence that would change the online medical information world forever.

In June 1991, a Japanese businessman donated $21,000 to the HIV/AIDS Info BBS, allowing me to invest in a more powerful IBM compatible computer with a 660-megabyte hard drive, two high-speed US Robotics modems, and two incoming phone lines. With the expanded capacity, the database mushroomed to more than 1,500 files. By year-end, the number of users had risen to more than 20,000.

About this time, I received a call from Jamie Jemison. Jamie had started the AIDS Education General Information Service (AEGiS) BBS while attending the University of California, Irvine (UCI). Jamie had the right idea: he was just too early. When Jamie started his BBS, home computers with modems were virtually non-existent. So, after a year, Jamie shut it down. I suggested that he restart the service, but he declined. Instead, he offered AEGiS to me, and I accepted.

I had started the process of incorporating as a 501(c)3 not-for-profit service. Chris Quilter, a new friend, was helping me. Chris mistakenly entered our name as AIDS Education Global Information System (AEGiS). The name fit, as we were now global thanks to FidoNet, and we were part of a network system. In 1992, AEGiS became a 501c(3) not-for-profit corporation, founded on the premise that, "Until there is a cure, there is AEGiS." In other words, information is the only effective weapon against AIDS.

One afternoon, John James, who published AIDS Treatment News, logged on. John spent about an hour checking out the scientific abstracts and news that I had acquired and put online. He logged off and logged back on about 10 minutes later and proceeded to upload every issue of his AIDS Treatment News.

I logged in and thanked him.

He replied, "I'm sorry I took so long to check you out. You are for real, and I want to thank you for your efforts to help."

Attitudes began to change after that, and the various AIDS organizations began to share their information with us. Up until then, the majority of the larger AIDS organizations were unwilling to share their information with us, nor were they interested in using our services.

The negativity that existed, in the beginning, was that a Sister ran AEGiS. The negativity began to disappear, thanks to the efforts of John James and Tomás Fábregas. Tomás played a crucial role in getting the San Francisco AIDS Foundation to allow AEGiS to publish their Bulletin of Experimental Treatments for AIDS (BETA) online. Tomás was a former board member of the organization. He told Lisa Krieger, a staff writer for the San Francisco Examiner:

Around the world, access to critical treatment information was being restricted by the very organization which has taken grant money—for providing it.

Lisa went on to write:

> *It didn't seem to matter that AEGiS was creating a vast free-access reference library, linked to more than 100 computer bulletin boards from all over the world, disseminating information from rural Minnesota to urban Jakarta, Indonesia, and everywhere in between.*

She told her readers:

> *AEGiS was also a cozy kaffeeklatsch where doctors and researchers talk about what's hot in their world long before it makes headlines."*

About this time, I also received a call from the National AIDS Policy Office (NAPO), at the White House asking could I come to Washington and assist them in establishing a BBS. I said I'd love to, but I didn't have the funds for such a trip. They told me that the White House would pay my way, and they'd also pay me $900 a day, which was the standard consultant's fee. The following Sunday, I flew to Washington and spent four days setting up a BBS for the NAPO.

The reality of the situation was that they had the skilled personnel who could have configured the NAPO BBS for them, but they were more interested in helping me. The $3600 consultant's fee would help me add an additional phone line, and it would also help pay my share of the monthly electric bill.

I told them to purchase eSoft's TBBS and TDBS software. It did not arrive in time for me to install and configure, so I installed my own copy of the software.

Figure 22: Sister Mary Elizabeth at AEGiS

I was sitting in the closet where the BBS would reside, waiting for a call from eSoft to provide me with the software activation codes. When I heard a cough behind me, I turned to see who it was, and there was Vice President Al Gore and Secretary of Health and Human

Services, Donna Shalala. I jumped from my chair and greeted them, "Vice President Gore, Secretary Shalala, how nice to see you."

Vice President Gore asked, "Who are you, and what are you doing sitting in the closet?"

I replied, "I'm Sister Mary Elizabeth, and I'm here installing the new NAPO AIDS BBS. The software didn't arrive in time, so I have installed my copy of the software, and I'm waiting on eSoft to call and give me your activation license codes."

Vice President Gore asked me, "Sister Mary Elizabeth, didn't you write to me a couple of weeks ago?"

"Yes, Sir, I did, and you resolved the problem." We chatted a bit, and then they left to attend a meeting.

The upcoming 1994 election (104th Congress) was going to become a disaster for the Democrats when both the Senate and House of Representatives came under Republican control. One bit of information they didn't want the Republicans to get hold of was the Sister, who had free access to Grateful-MED, and was giving the medical information away free to those in need.

Vice President Gore came to the rescue. He had been promoting the new Internet as an "Information Superhighway," and he suggested re-creating Grateful-MED as a web-based medical information resource on the "Internet," using the Ryan White Comprehensive AIDS Resources Emergency (CARE) Act of 1990 as a funding resource. PubMed went online in January 1996, providing free global access to MEDLINE®. That was the unintended consequence that changed the medical information world forever.

A few weeks later, I received a phone call from a representative at Sandler Communications, an advertising firm in New York. They wanted to know if I would accept funding from a pharmaceutical company. I said, "Yes," but I would have a few restrictions. I outlined my conditions, and the representative said that they shouldn't be a problem. He told me I would receive a call from Roxane Laboratories shortly.

About 20 minutes later, Tom Sawyer and Ian Wendt, representing Roxane Laboratories, a Boehringer Ingelheim subsidiary, called. They asked if we could meet the next day. I said, "Yes," and asked what time and where they were coming from.

Ian replied, "Columbus, Ohio, and we should be there by 10 am."

I called Chris, and he agreed to join me. The next morning, Tom and Ian arrived as expected at 10 am. We introduced ourselves, and then, I gave them a look at the BBS. Tom suggested we get an early lunch, so we drove down to the El Torito restaurant at the Dana Point Harbor. Over lunch, we had a question-and-answer session that ended with the big question.

"What will it cost to move everything to the Internet's World Wide Web?"

I replied, "$109,000 for the first year, and about "$65,000" per year after that."

We drove back to the house, and they asked where I would set up the Web server.

I pointed to the corner. "It will replace the BBS there."

Tom said, "Great."

Ian smiled and said, "You'll have a check tomorrow morning." There was no written contract, just a handshake, and trust.

After everyone departed, my father came in and asked how the meeting had gone.

I told him, "Great, they are going to send a check tomorrow for $109,000."

Dad responded, "They're pulling your leg. No one is going to give you $109,000."

Tom and Ian were true to their word, however, and FEDEX delivered the check on schedule the next morning.

I deposited the check, then headed up to Micro Center in Tustin to get the parts and software I would need to build our first server. After I returned home, I called the Internet provider in Los Angeles and scheduled them to come and install a T1 data line. It was going to cost $2,200 a month.

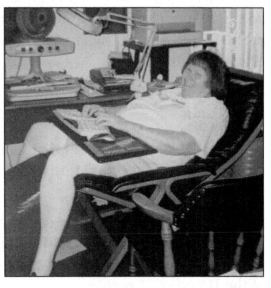

Figure 23: Joanna at her workstation

I got the server built but had to learn how to code in HTML. One of my BBS regulars offered to assist. Wynn Wagner was a professional programmer and was HIV positive. He flew out from Dallas, Texas, and spent a week designing the website and teaching me how to code.

Tom called and asked if they could borrow the server. They wanted to demonstrate it at a pharmaceutical conference. I agreed to ship it to them that afternoon. The conference went well, but the return was a disaster. FedEx cargo handlers dropped the server, and it fell from the aircraft cargo hatch to the ground. Scratch one server. FedEx paid for the replacement, and I, fortunately, had made a backup of the software installation. Our only loss was time.

I replaced the server, and AEGiS went live on the Internet. AEGIS.org was not available, so we launched as AEGIS.com. A year later, I saw that AEGIS.org had become available, and I was able to register it. A year later, we sold AEGIS.com to a security agency in Santa Ana. The change was necessary because ".com" indicates the company is a commercial, for-profit organization, whereas ".org" identifies non-profit organizations.

∾

Over the next four years, I ran the day-to-day operation of maintaining the server farm and database on my own, working a 16/7 schedule.[75]

In 1998, Betty Canepa came on-board as a volunteer fundraiser. She came on full-time after her husband passed away. She served as both full-time fundraiser and President of the Board of Directors.

One evening in 1999, Tom Sawyer called from Roxane Laboratories. He was checking in to see how I was doing. I

---

[75] 16 hours a day, 7 days a week.

told Tom, "AEGiS has gotten too big for one person. I need help."

Tom responded, "It's about time you admitted that. How much do you need?"

I said, "I don't know, maybe $50,000 to hire a couple of helpers."

Tom replied, "You'll have it tomorrow."

I spoke to Jeff Greer the next morning, and a week later, Jeff joined the team as Executive Director. Jeff had a degree in business administration, and he was very familiar with federal non-profit compliance issues. To join AEGiS, Jeff took early retirement and a hefty pay cut.

Funding began to come in thanks to the efforts of Betty Canepa and Jeff Greer. By year-end, we had received $50,000 from the Elton John Foundation, a recurring $25,000 grant from the National Library of Medicine, and an annual check from the Bridgestone/Firestone Foundation.

In April 2000, Jeff began to expand the staff, hiring Vanessa Robison as a data specialist. Vanessa had just had a baby, and she had brought him with her for her interview. As I bounced the baby on my knee, I told her I would hire her on one condition; that she bring the baby to work with her each day.

Over the next couple of months, Jeff brought Lisa Hoskins on board. The living room was becoming overcrowded, so I decided that I would move my workstation into my bedroom when Jeff hired the next assistant.

&

On December 27, 2001, I was still working in the living room. About 30 minutes before it was time to close up for the day, I heard my mother go out on the porch. She loved to sit there in the afternoon and enjoy the sun. At 4:30 pm, the staff closed down their stations, and I walked them out onto the porch. Vanessa was first out the door, and she turned and said goodbye to my mother, but my mother didn't respond. I walked over to check on her, and I found that she had passed away. She was 89 years old.

My father was out in the park delivering oranges, which grew on his tree in our back yard, to the neighbors. Vanessa called the paramedics. They arrived and moved my mother inside and wrote up a report—death due to old age and natural causes.

When I heard my father in the driveway, I went out to tell him. He came in, hugged and kissed her goodbye, and then sat down and waited. I had called the Neptune Society, and they arrived shortly and took Mom's body away.

Over the next couple of weeks, we brought April Ele on board, and I moved my station to my bedroom. It started to become clear that we were going to have to move to a business park. Our electric bill was now over $750 a month, and we were close to exceeding the maximum load limitation on our incoming power pedestal.

Dad discovered the perfect office on Paseo Adelanto. What was amazing was that we could look down the street from our kitchen window through a neighbor's carport directly into the front window of the office of what would become our new home.

Jeff and I secured the office, hired an electrician to wire what would become our new server room, and bring in a new T1 communications line. With that, we began the move. Those offices would be our home for the next year.

The AEGiS database continued to grow, and by year-end, we had logged 18 million user sessions. Unfortunately, some of our grants expired, and we were unable to replace them. Simultaneously, my father's health began to fail, and I had to spend more time at home caring for him.

Figure 24: Certificate of Special Congressional Recognition
"Women Making a Difference to Orange County
In Appreciation for Your Outstanding and Dedicated Service"

From our kitchen window, the line-of-sight path, down the street through the neighbor's carport into our front office window, was a lifesaver. I put in a microwave link and moved my workstation back to the house. In May 2004, we lost another grant, and it became clear we would have to abandon the office.

Figure 25: Certificates of Appreciation

Rather than move everyone back to the house, the staff shifted their workstations to their homes. We moved the servers back to the porch at my house and connected everyone through a wide-area network. The new arrangement worked well, and AEGiS continued to grow in size and number of users.

❧

In 2014, we lost a large segment of our funding. Fortunately, Jeff had managed to save enough of our budget to keep us online for a while provided we reduced our staff size. April was the first to leave. Jeff and I followed. Lisa moved to New Jersey and continued to work from there.

In August 2014, my father passed away. He was 93 years young. I could not have asked for better parents.

❧

We were unable to find adequate funding, so in May 2015, AEGiS had no choice. We had to close down. We had a good two and a half-decade run, and we did it on an annual budget that never exceeded $280,000 a year.

I tried to negotiate a deal with COX, our Internet provider, to keep the database online. COX, however, was not willing to donate our Internet connection in exchange for a tax deduction.

I offered copies of the database to existing AIDS groups. iBase in the United Kingdom and the University of California, San Francisco requested copies. I also send a copy to the National Institute of Health and the National Library of Medicine.

It was time to move on.

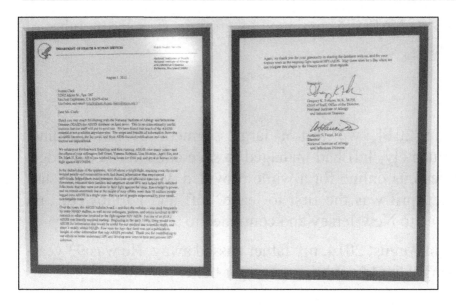

***Figure 26: Letter of Commendation from Gregory Folkers and
Anthony Fauci of the National Institute of Allergy and Infectious
Diseases***
Note: Text of letter follows

August 1, 2015

Dear Ms. Clark:

*Thank you very much for sharing with the National
Institute of Allergy and Infectious Diseases (NIAID)
the AEGiS database on hard drive. This is an
extraordinarily useful resource that our staff will
put to good use. We have found that much of the
AEGiS material is not available anywhere else. The
scope and breadth of information from the scientific
literature, the lay press, and from AIDS-focused
publication and other sources are unparalleled.*

We salute your tireless work founding, and then running, AEGiS over many years—and the efforts of your colleagues Jeff Greer, Vanessa Robison, Lisa Hoskins, April Ele, and Dr. Mark H. Katz. All of you worked long hours for little pay and are true heroes in the fight against HIV-AIDS.

In the darkest days of the epidemic, AEGiS shone a bright light reaching even the most isolated people and communities with fact-based information that empowered individuals, helped them make treatment decisions, and otherwise take care of themselves, educate their families and neighbors about HIV, and helped HIV-infected folks know that they were not alone in their fight against the virus. Knowledge is power, and we remain awestruck that at the height of your efforts more than 18 million people logged onto AEGiS in a single year—that is a lot of people empowered by your small indefatigable team.

Over the years, the AEGiS bulletin board—and then the website—was used frequently by many NIAID staffers, as well as our colleagues, patients, and others involved in HIV research or otherwise involved in the fight against HIV/AIDS. For one of us (G.F.), AEGiS was literally required reading. Beginning in the early 1990s, Greg would scan AEGiS for information that would be useful for our medical and scientific staffs and share it widely within NIAID. Few were the days that there was not a publication, insight, or other information that only AEGiS provided. Thank you for contributing to our efforts to better understand HIV and develop new ways to treat and prevent HIV infection.

Again, we thank you for your generosity in sharing the database with us, and for your tireless work in the ongoing fight against HIV-AIDS. May there soon be a day when we can relegate this plague to the history books. Best regards.

Sincerely,

Gregory K. Folkers, M.S., M.PH.
Chief of Staff, Office of the Director,
National Institute of Allergy
 and Infectious Diseases

Anthony S. Fauci, M.D.
Director
National Institute of Allergy
 and Infectious Diseases

A New Beginning

AEGiS officially closed down the website on 15 May 2015, ending two and a half decades working 16/7 with the AIDS pandemic, and it was clear that I had some catching up to do with what was going on in the world. What would be next on my agenda? There was a raging ongoing debate over global warming and climate change.

Were the effects of global warming and climate change as bad on the environment as the climate scientists claimed? If they were, then, clearly, they were worth consideration.

Figure 27: Bookcase with models of planes and awards

The scientific consensus was that global warming *is* real and human-caused. Repeated analysis of peer-reviewed scientific journals by different groups similarly showed that 97 to 100 percent of actively publishing climate scientists agreed: global warming *is* real and human-caused. The most extensive review analyzed 13,950 peer-reviewed research reports published between 1991 and 2012. It found that of the 13,950 peer-reviewed reports, only 24 (<0.2%) rejected anthropogenic global warming. That's 581:1, in case you are a gambler.

Over the next two years, I filled eight bookcases with peer-reviewed science journals and books on global warming and climate change. The more I read, the more convinced I became. We have a problem.

The lack of concern among my generation is beyond comprehension, but there is hope. Our youth have recognized the gravity of the situation we face, and they are inspiring others to get involved.

Six-year-old Xiuhtezcatl Martinez was one of the youngest environmental activists when he spoke at the National Global Warming Event in 1986, while 12-year-old Severn Cullis Suzuki made an impassioned plea to avert ecological disaster at the Rio de Janeiro Earth Summit in 1992. I credit Xiuhtezcatl and Severn for my initial decision to commit myself to environmental activism and Greta Thunberg for kick-starting me into high gear.

৵

Six months after AEGiS closed its doors, the world gathered in Paris and agreed to avoid the worst impacts of climate change by limiting global temperature increases to 2°C above pre-industrial levels by the end of the century. Like earlier international meetings, there was pushback by the "Merchants of Doubt."[76]

The U.N. Intergovernmental Panel on Climate Change (IPCC) issued their Special Report "Global Warming of 1.5°C" in November 2018.[77] It gave us 12 years, or until 2030, to limit devastating global warming. A week later, the congressionally mandated US Global Change Research Program's 4th National Climate Assessment was published. It gave us 12 years, as well. Twelve years means we have until 2030—*12 years or 2030*—to keep global warming to a maximum of 1.5°C, beyond which even half a degree will significantly worsen the risks of drought, floods, extreme heat, and millions of people living in poverty.

Despite the science, the Congressional naysayers repeatedly state that, despite the accumulated evidence, they do not believe we puny humans can have a global effect on climate. They say that it is strictly a natural cycle of freeze and melt. But one only has to look at human history: it could not be more precise. We have a history of altering the planet's climate on massive scales: ongoing desertification due to deforestation, the dust bowl in the US in the 1930s, the severe smog of the '40s, '50s, '60s, and '70s, or the ozone hole of the 1970s.

---

[76] See https://en.wikipedia.org/wiki/Merchants_of_Doubt.

[77] See https://www.ipcc.ch/sr15/.

The Paris agreement called for countries to come together every five years, most recently in November 2020. Unfortunately, with the arrival of the COVID-19 pandemic, the November 2020 Glasgow conference was postponed to November 2021.

Figure 28: Joanna with pictures of women astronauts
Photo credit: Margot Wilson

President Donald Trump, a non-believer in science, announced on 1 June 2017 that the United States would cease all participation in the 2015 Paris Agreement because of what he believed to be an unfair economic burden. The withdrawal took effect one year from the delivery of the official withdrawal notification.

People don't seem able to grasp that the two primary climate science reports, published in 2018, gave us 12 years (until 2030)—not 2035, 2050, or 2060. More than 110 countries have set net-zero targets for mid-century. Unfortunately, we do not have until mid-century to save the planet.

ॐ

This past October (2020), Severn, still involved in climate change concerns, gave a TED Talk, where she reminded us that "History has shown us that in moments of crisis, society can truly transform."

Xiuhtezcatl has traveled the world establishing Earth Guardian youth groups to fight to save the environment for future generations. In 2015, 21 youth, and organizational plaintiff Earth Guardians, filed their constitutional climate lawsuit, *Juliana v. United States*, against the US government. US District Judge Ann Aiken wrote, "Exercising my 'reasoned judgment,' I have no doubt that the right to a climate system capable of sustaining human life is fundamental to a free and ordered society."[78]

Recently, Xiuhtezcatl and Severn have been joined by Greta Thunberg, Time Magazine's "2020 Person of the Year," and others, inspiring us to take a stand against Climate Change.

Today, I share my life with Ana Sandoval. We drive an electric vehicle (EV), have replaced all of our incandescent and fluorescent lights with LEDs, and hope to go solar by the end of 2021. I spend much of my time on environmental issues, working with fellow Sierra Club members and the Citizen's Climate Lobby. I don't know how successful we will be, but I do know that, like the crew of Apollo 13, "Houston, we have a problem." NASA and the crew worked together to solve that problem, and the crew returned safely to earth. If we can put our differences aside and work

---

[78] See https://www.resilience.org/stories/2021-02-16/juliana-v-us-children-standing-at-the-crossroads/.

together, we can solve our problems and save the future. We've done it before, and we will do it again.

I hope you will join us. Until then, stay tuned.

It is difficult to say what is impossible, for the dream of yesterday is the hope of today and the reality of tomorrow.

Robert Hutchings Goddard
Visionary rocket scientist

Afterword

It is my hope that in time science will unravel the mysteries of how our identity forms, followed by a simple test to confirm our true identity. That could end years of suffering.

A child tells their parents, "Hey, Mom, Dad, I know you didn't expect this, but I really feel that I'm a boy, not a girl," or "I feel that I'm a girl, not a boy." "Can we ask the doctor to check."

Then, we could raise the child in accordance with their gender.

Wouldn't that be great?

Joanna Clark
March 2021

Other Publications from Castle Carrington Publishing Group

Other Life Stories Available from TransGender Publishing
Publishing Transgender Life Stories and Non-fiction
https://transgenderpublishing.ca/

TRANScestors: Navigating LGBTQ+ Aging, Illness and End of Life Decisions (2020)
Volume I: Generations of Hope
Edited by Jude Patton and Margot Wilson
This volume (and the ones that follow) have been in the works for some time. What finally emerges after many months of assiduous advertising, recruiting, editing, and organizing is a volume of intimate, nuanced, and heartfelt stories that reflect the wide diversity in the ways in which trans, non-binary, and Two-Spirit people have come to recognize, signify, embody, and celebrate their difference as their authentic selves. Moreover, with an increasing emphasis on the experiences of trans youth, elders constitute a routinely overlooked, disregarded, and/or silenced segment of the community. In response, this volume documents the myriad ways in which trans elders are coming to terms with the real-life challenges of aging, illness, and end of life decision-making.

TRANScestors is planned as a series of edited volumes that address the issues of LGBTQ+ aging, illness, and end of life decision-making and will be published by TransGender Publishing. Additional volumes include: Volume II: Generations of Change, Volume III: Generations of Pride, and Volume III: Generations of Challenge. https://transgenderpublishing.ca/life-trips/

TRANScestors: Navigating LGBTQ+ Aging, Illness and End of Life Decisions (2020)
Volume II: Generations of Change
Edited by Jude Patton and Margot Wilson
Generations of Change is the second volume in the TRANScestors series. These stories are, by turn, heartfelt, revealing, inspiring, sad, joyful, humorous, irreverent, and incredibly varied. And yet, strong, common themes of courage, persistence, honesty, resilience, and authenticity emerge clearly through the detailed recounting of the individual lives lived. Each author details those specific circumstances that have led them to the places and situations in which they find themselves today. On the whole, these are places of comfort, confidence, revelation, and affirmation. The wide range of attitudes, expressions, and worldviews held by the LGBTQ+ elders presented here challenge us all to carefully consider and adjust our perspectives on our own aging processes and, ultimately, on finding our own places in the world. (https://transgenderpublishing.ca/live-trips-vol-ii-generations-of-change/)

We are God's Children Too (2020)
Rona Matlow
At the heart of Jewish experience is narrative. Around the dinner table, we tell stories of our families, recalling the quality of a grandmother's cooking, the kindness (or stinginess) of a particular uncle, the ways in which traditions have developed and shifted in our families. In synagogues and Jewish schools, we read the Torah, which is filled with stories of our religious patriarchs and matriarchs. And then there are the stories of Diaspora–the history of Jewish communities existing in exile for over two millennia. There are family stories and history books dedicated to our many wanderings. All of these stories help Jewish people connect to their heritage and lineage. What of the queer Jew? Even as more and more Jewish communities emphasize inclusivity and find a place for queer congregants, Jewish stories do not. The Bible offers no queer lessons, leaving queer Jews split in two; a Jewish heritage and a queer present. Enter Rabbah Rona Matlow, with hir queer *midrashim*. *Midrashim* are stories which approach Biblical texts from new perspectives, often exploring areas of confusion or possible contradiction within the Bible. Unlike Torah, they are not presented as factual, but as possibilities. Fictions which might yet be

possible alternate histories. *Midrashim* bridge gaps. Rona's queer *midrashim* bridge the gap between the contemporary queer Jew and the (seemingly cisgender and straight) Bible, offering a way for us to see ourselves in our Jewish tradition.
(https://transgenderpublishing.ca/we-are-gods-children-too/)

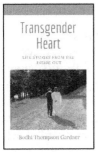

Transgender Heart: Life Stories from the Inside Out (2020)
Bodhi Thompson Gardner
Transgender Heart is a collection of short stories that trace the heart-journey of a small farm kid, youth, and adult, from rural Saskatchewan, across the binary landscapes of life. A deeply grateful soul emerges, while exploring all the hidden nuances of the people, places, and things that held them together. Hidden comforts are revealed from the inside out, an inner harvesting of an authentic self. Their true self searching for somewhere to belong, finds love, acceptance, and authentic connection in the most intriguing and unusual spaces. Black hockey skates not only enrich their game but authenticate their heart. Spaces of unconditional love come from four-legged wild beasts, two-legged mentors, matriarchs, warriors, and elders. An RCMP officer who saw their struggle and offered a hand instead of handcuffs, gifts of nature, and family support abound: however, the biggest surprise of all is their most cherished treasure, the one thing that kept them alive for over 50 years. Transgender Heart highlights the courage and tenacity of the human spirit to rise up!
(https://transgenderpublishing.ca/transgender-heart/)

QdQh: Queen of Diamonds, Queen of Hearts, The Life and Journey of Michelle Nastasis, the First Known Transgender Professional Poker Player (2020)
Michelle Nastasis
QdQh: Queen of Diamonds, Queen of Hearts is the life story of Michelle Nastasis, the First Known Transgender Professional Poker Player.™ Michelle is courageous whether going head-to-head with the best poker players in the world, speaking out on television for LGBTQ+ rights, or marching in parades to celebrate being transgender. She is calm, cool, collected, and absolutely fearless. Possessed of fierce intelligence, Michelle is a beacon for younger transgender people. She shoots straight from the hip. She's blunt, loud, sarcastic, and occasionally irreverent. So, sit back and enjoy the ride.

(https://transgenderpublishing.ca/misunderstood/)

Glimmerings: Trans Elders Tell Their Stories (2019)
Margot Wilson and Aaron Devor (editors)

Tell us your story. A story about growing up before the age of global communication, at a time when the Internet and worldwide connectivity were still visions of the future; when inflexible, dichotomous categories of male and female, men and women, existed; when heterosexuality was the only sanctioned form of romantic attraction or sexual conduct; and when any expression of interest outside of these strict prescriptions was severely censured. Tell us your story about living in a time when those whose preferences, perspectives, and behaviours contravened the prevailing paradigms and prohibitions, when you had to negotiate dark, prejudicial places where fear, shame, guilt, despair, isolation, and a little bit of hope. Contributing authors include: Stephanie Castle, Joanna Clark, Ms. Bob Davis, Dallas Denny, Jamison Green, Ariadne Kane, Corey Keith, Lili, Ty Nolan, Jude Patton, Virginia Prince, Rupert Raj, Gayle Roberts, Susanna Valenti, and Dawn Angela Wensley.
(https://transgenderpublishing.ca/glimmerings-recognition-authenticity-and-gender-variance/)

Dancing the Dialectic: True Tales of a Transgender Trailblazer, Second Edition (2020)
Rupert Raj

Rupert Raj is a trailblazing, Eurasian-Canadian, trans activist, and former psychotherapist, who transitioned from female to male in 1971 as a transsexual teenager. Dancing the dialectic between gender dysphoria and gender euphoria, cynical despair and realistic hope, righteous rage and loving kindness, this Gender Worker tells us all about his lifelong fight for the rights of transgender, intersex, and two-spirit people—and his later-life role as a Rainbow Warrior working to free Mother Earth's enslaved animals.
(https://transgenderpublishing.ca/dancing-the-dialectic-true-tales-of-a-transgender-trailblazer-second-edition/)

My Untrue Past: The Coming of Age of a Trans Man (2019)
Alex Bakker

Born the youngest daughter in a small-town family in the Netherlands, Alex Bakker underwent gender reaffirming transition when he was twenty-eight years old. A new beginning, in the right body, he literally put everything that reminded him of his old life into boxes, never to be opened again. More than fifteen years later, he has finally gathered the courage to face his past. In *My Untrue Past*, Alex goes in search of the painful truth. What does it mean to be betrayed by your body, to be immensely jealous of boys, and to decide that everything needs to be different? (https://transgenderpublishing.ca/my-untrue-past-available-now/)

Girl in the Dream: Stephanie (Sydney) Castle Heal, a Transgender Life (2018)
Margot E. Wilson

Girl in the Dream is the life story of Stephanie (Sydney) Castle Heal, an advocate, activist and elder in the Canadian transgender community. The outcome of an almost four-year collaboration of storytelling, recording, analysis, and writing, *Girl in the Dream* is a first-person narrative that depicts in intimate detail Stephanie's transgender journey. An enthusiastic and accomplished raconteuse, Stephanie tells her story with the verve, passion, and expressiveness of a veteran storyteller. https://transgenderpublishing.ca/girl-in-the-dream/)

Feelings: A Transsexual's Explanation of a Baffling Condition, Second Edition (2018)
Stephanie Castle
Edited and Introduction by Margot E. Wilson

Feelings is written in a style that reveals Stephanie Castle as a woman of great confidence, conviction and humour. It reflects her attitudes toward life in general and transgender issues in particular, and definitively emulates the intricacies of her personality and character. *Feelings* provides a very personal view into one transgender woman's journey, a metamorphosis that is as vital, authentic and significant today as it was when she wrote it. A complementary volume to *Girl in the Dream*, *Feelings* provides a comprehensive and in-depth view into the nature of the transgender experience based on the intimate, challenging, and often poignant experiences and perspectives of one singularly remarkable woman. (https://transgenderpublishing.ca/feelings/)

Available now from
Castle Carrington Publishing
You have a story. Let us help you tell it.
https://castlecarringtonpublishing.ca/

PUBLICATION EXPECTED IN 2020
Until I Smile at You (2020)
How one girl's heartbreak electrified Frank Sinatra's fame!
Peter Jennings with Tom Sandler
It's 1936. Take Ina Ray Hutton, the "Blonde Bombshell of Rhythm," add 22-year-old Ruth Lowe, who become Ina Ray's pianist. Ruth marries music publicist Harold Cohen, but he dies in the midst of debilitating surgery. Ruth is devastated, full of heartache, a grief-stricken widow far too early. Consumed by anguish, she pours her heartache into a lamenting anthem that becomes an internationally famous song—"I'll Never Smile Again"—destined to electrify the career of 25-year-old vocalist Francis Albert Sinatra. Ruth next composes what becomes Sinatra's theme song, "Put Your Dreams Away." And then, Act Two begins for Ruth Lowe: she withdraws from the limelight to become a caring wife, loving mother, society doyenne, and friend to many. Amazingly, this superstar has escaped the investigation and adoration that her life so richly deserves—until now.
(https://castlecarringtonpublishing.ca/until-i-smile-at-you/)

Ruth's Wonderful Song: A Story for Kids (2021)
Peter Jennings
Ruth's Wonderful Song is a true story of a young woman who loved to play her bright yellow piano. She wrote a wonderful song that people are still listening to more than 80 years after she wrote it. Tom, Ruth's son, tells the story of how Ruth wrote her wonderful song and what happened next.

(https://castlecarringtonpublishing.ca/ruths-wonderful-song/)

A Lion in Waiting (2021)
H.W. Coyle

While serving as an observer with the British Expeditionary Force in 1940, Ian Wylie survives a massacre of prisoners. In its aftermath, he resolves to find a way of sitting out the rest of the war, safe from both the Germans and his responsibilities. At first, he finds sanctuary on a small farm owned by a teacher, Andrea Morel, who harbours him until an incident leaves her no choice but to send Ian away. With no wish to return to England and the war, Ian assumes the identity of Andrea's sister, Diane Lambert, and accepts an offer to teach at a Catholic girls' school in Normandy. His efforts to turn his back on the war are frustrated by a local businessman who enlists Ian's aid in passing intelligence on German activities in Normandy to the Allies as well as by a group of schoolgirls who take it upon themselves to fight for the liberation of France. (https://stephaniecastle.ca/a-lion-in-waiting/)

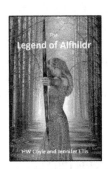

The Legend of Alfhildr (2020)
HW. Coyle and Jennifer Ellis

For generations, a legend spoke of a young Viking girl who led a Saxon-Dane army against a usurper. The story was passed from storyteller to storyteller, who freely embellished the feats of Alfhildr as they sought to entertain and enthrall their audiences in the great halls of their lords and masters. Some claimed she had been raised by a wolf, others that she was a witch. The truth was vastly different.

But before she became a legend, Alfhildr was a flesh and blood person with a family, a past, and a secret. With the passing of time, all but the legend was lost from living memory until an archeologist stumbles upon something he has not been expecting. Bit by bit, Professor Bannon and his students come to realize that the legend once thought to be little more than a myth could be grounded in history. He also begins to suspect one of the students participating in the dig has a secret that links her to both the discoveries they are making and the legend. (https://stephaniecastle.ca/legend-of-alfhildr/)

Flipping (2020)
It cost him nothing, but it cost her everything.
Forest J. Handford

Born on a space station, Samir Zeka was raised Muslim, observes a Halal diet, fasts during Ramadan, and prays 5 times every day. An introvert, he mostly stuck to his work, his home, his family, and his church community, until the day he decided to push beyond his comfort zone and attend a party that would forever change his life. Intending to look his best for the party, Samir searched his neural link "mesh" for random looks until he came across one that suited him. After some fine-tuning, he "flipped" to the persona of Samantha, a late 30s East Asian, cat-eared woman with shoulder-length purple hair. At the party, Samantha meets Anna, someone who will change Samantha's perceptions of herself and transform both of their lives.
(https://stephaniecastle.ca/flipping/)

The Elysian Project: A Story of Betrayal and Payback (2019)
D. Axt

The Elysian Project is an expertly written, fast paced action thriller with a twist. It follows US marine scout sniper, Brent chandler, his surviving teammate, Lyle, and his adopted father (the Gunny), as they go after those responsible for betraying Brent's sniper team during a military operation in Haditha, Iraq. Chandler's betrayal didn't just change the lives of his US Marine sniper team forever. It set him on a path of unimaginable discovery. His quest for the truth and revenge quickly goes awry, drawing the attention of billionaire Stanley Tivador and the DOJ-FBI cabal he controls. The chase is on, from northern Minnesota's Superior National Forest to the Canary Islands. With help from the Gunny, his crotchety, retired Marine father, and Staiski, his friend and former sniper teammate, Chandler uncovers a terrorist plot of carnage inconceivable in magnitude and in lives lost. With seconds remaining, they risk everything to stop The Elysian Project.
(https://stephaniecastle.ca/the-elysian-project/)

Partnership: A Novel about Friendship, Love, Family and Gender Transition (2019)
Stephanie Castle
Edited and preface by Margot Wilson
What happens when a lawyer, the son of a prominent Vancouver family, and a baker, the son of a devoted Catholic family who moved from Italy to Montreal following WWII, team up while going through gender reassignment? This humorous, yet serious, depiction of two families coping with gender dysphoria and the challenges of keeping family relationships intact addresses both legal and religious issues. The depiction and commentary on a range of human personalities in the hands of the author are both perceptive and entertaining. The underlying accuracy of this fictional story depends on the author's personal experience as a transgender woman and as a counselor in the transgender community in Vancouver.
(https://stephaniecastle.ca/partnership/)

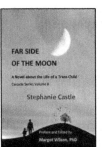

Far Side of the Moon: A Novel about the Life of a Trans Child (2019)
Stephanie Castle
Edited and preface by Margot Wilson
In Far Side of the Moon, Marjorie Burton and her husband, Jack, demonstrate all the attributes needed to help their child, Jenna, through a successful male to female gender transition. For children raised in an era when the condition of gender dysphoria was unknown, when anything unusual or unexplained was written off as a sexual aberration, it is small wonder that children, like the author, kept their feelings hidden out of shame and fear. Fortunately, that is not what happens with Jenna.
(https://stephaniecastle.ca/far-side-of-the-moon-a-novel-about-the-life-of-a-trans-child/)

Now Available from
Perceptions Press
Publishing innovative, avant-garde (and occasionally provocative) transgender fiction and non-fiction
https://perceptionspress.ca/

7 Minutes (2021)
Will2Love Series Book 2
Paul Van Der Spiegel

At the point of death,
lost to all we've known,
adrift from those we've loved,
what stories do we tell
ourselves?

7 Minutes is the story of a death—charting the progress from cardiac arrest, the brain's release of its massive reserve of endorphins, through the unravelling of personality, memory, and identity as the brain's consciousness-generating areas are hit by a tidal wave of opioid neuropeptides that are simultaneously being starved of oxygen.

Self-told narratives unfold and are re-contextualised, fears awaken, desires awaken, time is warped and regresses as the mind is trapped inside a dead husk, unable to communicate, lost to those it has loved and been loved by.

Those who have experienced so-called 'near death' experiences have described bright lights, meeting loved ones: but no-one has returned from behind that light to describe the process of dying. And so, we are left with either a gospel of redemption and condemnation, or its opposite, a gospel of cosmic resignation and the final extinction of personality. One day, perhaps not too far away, we shall know—or, then again, perhaps not.

7 Minutes is the collage of stories and half-truths that our protagonists' collapsing neural networks narrate as the brain asphyxiates—light and dark, fact and fiction, actuality and narrative—until the final arrival at the truth of an earthly existence. *7 Minutes* is a head fuck. But after you've read it, I hope you can celebrate being alive. (https://perceptionspress.ca/7-minutes/)

Demon of Want (2020)
Freja Ki Gray

Izumi Yamakawa, a directionless twenty-something, is a part-time employee of the Oh Joy Toy Store. When she witnesses her manager die in a horrific merchandising accident, she discovers that he was a member of a Japanese demon hunting organization and had been eyeing her for recruitment due to her family lineage. Now Izumi, along with her trans girlfriend Maria, and a boisterous sword-for-hire, Rhea, get caught up investigating the various monsters and demons running the Oh Joy Toy company. Demon of Want is an eclectic blend of tongue in cheek urban fantasy, over the top violence, and gratuitous sex.
https://perceptionspress.ca/demon-of-want/

Trans Deus (2020)
Will2Love Series Book 1
Paul Van Der Spiegel
In the beginning was the Verb,
the Verb was with God, the Verb was God.
In her was life,
that life was the light for all people.
The Verb was made trans woman
and she lived amongst us, full of grace and truth.
Her light shone in the darkness,
and the consumer-military-technocracy
comprehended it not.
We cast our votes on TV remotes,
crucified her live on Channel Five.
(https://perceptionspress.ca/trans-deus/)

Can't Her Bury Tales: A Transfeminine
Coloring Book (2020)
Iona Isabella Rivera
Hail weary traveler! Come closer! I don't bite…hard.
You lookit poorly, come take a sit by the fire. Rest and
grab yourself some stew I got cookin. Tell me, what
brings ya my way? Adventure? Hearsay? Curiosity or
plain ol' boredom? Well, no matter whence you came, I
surely have a story that will peak your delight.
Perhaps a tale of a terrible tragedy? Or a catty, Communist comedy? How
about some lore on fallin in love? Or a heroic tale of harrowing a horrible
governorship? Or be you one that pines over Power? Maybe a familiar fable
of family? Oh! Pardon my rambling. Come tell me your tale, traveler. What
colors will you paint with me? Tell, was your way hard, rocky and steep? Show
me. Perchance our stories crossed at some point. After all, we have more in
common than our differences tell.
(https://perceptionspress.ca/cant-her-bury-tales/)

Coming in 2021/2022 from
TransGender Publishing
Publishing Transgender Life Stories and Non-fiction
https://transgenderpublishing.ca/

PUBLICATION EXPECTED IN 2021/22
Life Trips: Navigating LGBTQ+ Aging, Illness and End of Life
Decisions
Edited by Jude Patton and Margot Wilson
Volume One: Generations of Hope
Volume Two: Generations of Change
Volume Three: Generations of Pride
Volume Four: Generations of Challenge
Studies indicate that LGBT+ people are still discriminated against in most
health care settings and in long term care facilities despite advances made in
the past few years in gaining more rights. Evaluating physical and mental
health care needs, facilitating access to health care providers and advocating
for clients' right as well as end of life decisions and planning for personal
legacy options are important aspects of navigating LGBTQ+ aging. Having
served as a health navigator for clients with chronic illness and offering end of
life doula services to LGBTQ+ community members, Jude Patton collaborates
with and advocates for his clients to successfully manage their health care
needs. Jude is a proud, open and out, elder trans man, who has worked with
under-served populations for most of his career, including LGBTQ+ folks,
geriatric clients, developmentally disabled adults, homeless/chronically
mentally ill and drug addicted clients. *Life Trips* is planned as a series of edited
volumes that address the issues of LGBTQ+ aging, illness, and end of life
decision-making and will be published by TransGender Publishing. Additional
volumes include: Volume II: Generations of Change, Volume III: Generations
of Pride and Volume IV: Generations of Challenge.
(https://transgenderpublishing.ca/life-trips/)

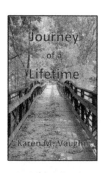

PUBLICATION EXPECTED IN 2021
Journey of a Lifetime
Karen Vaughn

For all of her life, Karen has struggled with gender dysphoria and her true identity. Frightened, confused, and tired of living a lie, she embarks on a journey—one that will change her life, her marriage, and the world she thought she knew. This is her story of coming to terms with who she really is, her struggles to find her way, and the life-altering changes that came along with her journey.
(https://transgenderpublishing.ca/journey-of-a-lifetime/)

PUBLICATION EXPECTED IN 2021
A Trans Feminist's Past
Forest Handford

Forest's memoir covers details of her life and the historical context in which it has been lived. Many of the stories in this book reveal the challenges of being feminine. While those challenges were painful, and some aspects of transitioning during her midlife were difficult, she values the views she has had on both sides of male privilege. She uses this rare perspective as an analogy for her understanding of white privilege.

While many trans stories exist, Forest's perspectives as an Eagle Scout, as somebody who lived in Egypt, and someone who transitioned while in a management position, bring new dimensions to the space, further illustrating that there is no single trans narrative.
(https://transgenderpublishing.ca/a-trans-feminists-past/)

PUBLICATIONS EXPECTED IN 2021
Triple Trans: One Woman's Journey to Freedom
Rose Barkimer

For me, *Triple Trans* means:

Transgender, the knowledge that one has been born with the incorrect physical body,

Transverse myelitis, a neurological affliction that was a catalyst in my decision to change gender and,

Transition, the process of change.

It is my hope that *Triple Trans* finds its way to at least one individual who is wrestling with the conundrum that is gender dysphoria and that my story helps them to understand their own journey. I also hope that my story will explain to the general public the experiences of one transgender individual and

demonstrate that, despite our differences, we are all human beings struggling with life's journey.
(https://transgenderpublishing.ca/triple-trans-one-womans-journey-to-freedom/)

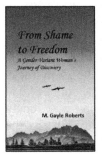

PUBLICATION EXPECTED IN 2021
From Shame to Freedom: A Gender Variant Woman's Journey of Discovery
M. Gayle Roberts

Born in England during WW II, Gayle Roberts immigrated to Canada in 1951 and is an UVic alumnus with an MSc in Physics. She transitioned in 1996 as her high school's Science Department Head and science teacher. Gayle coauthored the guidebook Supporting Transgender and Transsexual Students in K-12 Schools and is author of *From Shame to Freedom: A Gender-Variant Woman's Journey of Discovery*. Gayle feels strongly that trans individuals should document their life experiences. She utilizes specific literary writing techniques (creative nonfiction) to create factually accurate narratives. *From Shame to Freedom* is one of those narratives.
(https://transgenderpublishing.ca/from-shame-to-freedom/)

PUBLICATION EXPECTED IN 2022
Taking Care of Angela
Angela Wensley and Margot Wilson

My name is Angela, and I am a transsexual woman. I have always believed myself to be female, even though I spent the first forty-two years of my life being socialized as a male. To be transsexual is no longer a new phenomenon, although many misconceptions still surround it. One thing has remained unchanged is the great pain and personal upheaval that necessarily accompanies the transition from one gender to another. Looking back now, many years after having had gender reassignment surgery, it seems impossible for me to have accomplished what I have. Changing from man to woman involved no less than a total restructuring of every single relationship in my life, with my spouse, family, friends, workplace, and my everyday interactions in society. For me, being transsexual is a beautiful gift, an honour, an evolutionary jump, as it were, to a higher state of being, one in which I am closer to God and to all humanity.

My personal journey can be likened to casting off in a boat without oars into a swiftly flowing river. Standing on the banks of that river, intrigued but not knowing where it would lead me, I had dipped my toes into the water, even waded out to where it was deeper, where I could feel the tug of the current. How I longed to be swept away by the river: however, my fears kept me from the test and I always retreated to the security of the shore. Ultimately, spying a rowboat on the riverbank, I climbed in, pushed off into the stream, and waited as the small craft inevitably became caught up in the stronger current of mid-stream. Without oars, I could not return to where I had started and had little ability to control my course, though my direction downstream was certain. I was little prepared for the swiftness of the current, or the treacherous rapids and canyons that lay downstream out of sight. How easy it would have been to flounder in a back-eddy or to wreck on the many rocks that projected from the dark waters. Fortunately, with what little control I had over my course, I avoided destruction and travelled the long and lonely distance. Finally, one day, the current slowed, and I found myself past the mouth of the river, in the ocean that is woman.

https://transgenderpublishing.ca/taking-care-of-angela/

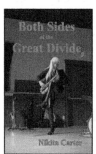

PUBLICATIONS EXPECTED OM 2021
Both Sides of the Great Divide
Nikita Carter
Nikita Carter tells her story about awakening. At 60 years of age, a series of shattering experiences led to her being broken open to the awareness that she was a trans woman, and she had to make the changes in her life to reflect that truth.

Her life has comprised extraordinary experiences and people throughout, which includes being a musician, composer, educator, Artistic Director, producer, and trans woman.
(https://transgenderpublishing.ca/both-sides-of-the-great-divide/)

PUBLICATION EXPECTED IN 2021
Gender Odyssey: Journey of an Intrepid Androgyne
Ariadne (J. Ari) Kane and Margot Wilson
Ariadne (J. Ari) Kane is a gerontology specialist with Theseus Consulting & Coaching Service. (S)he has developed several workshops focusing on issues of gender, sexuality and health in the latter decades of the lifespan. Many are designed for the LGBT Community. (S)he has been a leading authority on gender diversity in postmodern America and has given presentations at many universities and institutes in the United States and Canada. (S)he is one of the creators of the Gender Attitude Reassessment

Program, a workshop on gender for sexologists and healthcare professionals. (S)he co-authored *Crossing Sexual Boundaries* with Professor Vern Bullough. *Gender Odyssey: Journey of an Intrepid Androgyne* is the distillation of 40+ hours of recorded conversation that provide a decadal representation of an intrepid traveler who has forged an idiosyncratic path through gender exploration, variance and expression. (https://transgenderpublishing.ca/gender-odyssey-journey-of-an-intrepid-androgyne/)

PUBLICATION EXPECTED IN 2022
Young Kid, Old Goat: Transgender Journey to Understanding the Man Within
Jude Patton and Margot Wilson
Jude Patton is an elder transman and LGBTQ activist, advocate and educator since before his own transition in 1970. He founded Renaissance Gender Identity Services in the early 1970s and began publishing *Renaissance Newsletter* in the mid-1970s. Jude started one of the first informal support groups for FTM men and incorporated these into The John Augustus Foundation. Joined by Joanna Clark, these became known as J2CP Information Services, taking over Paul Walker's work with Erickson Educational Services. In *Young Kid, Old Goat*, Jude's personal life story and ongoing work is highlighted. (https://transgenderpublishing.ca/young-kid-old-goat/)

PUBLICATION EXPECTED IN 2022
Unconditional Love: Stories of LGBTQ+ People and Our Emotional Bonds with Companion Animals
Edited by Jude Patton and Margot Wilson
Our experiences with marginalization often affect our feelings of self-worth. While many people in our lives are unable (or unwilling) to provide the emotional support we need before, during and post-coming out, or transition, our companion animals never fail to see us as we truly are and never fail to express their unconditional love for us. No wonder we love them and derive multiple benefits from our relationships with them. They are woven into the fabric of our lives. *Unconditional Love* is planned as an edited reader that tells the stories of how the unconditional love of (and for) our companion animals has supported, encouraged, confirmed, validated, endorsed and sanctioned our authentic selves. Our reading audience includes those in the LGBTQ+

community who have found sanctuary and validation in the love shared with our animal companions as well as those in the broader community who revel in the company of our non-human loved ones.
(https://transgenderpublishing.ca/unconditional-love/)

**Coming in 2021/2022 from
Stephanie Castle Publications**
Publishing Transgender Fiction
https://transgenderpublishing.ca/

**PUBLICATION EXPECTED IN 2021
Tips
Newly Chronicles: Volume I
H.W. Coyle**
College is a time of discovery, when students find out just what sort of people they are. This is especially true for Andy Newly, a freshman who embarks on a unique journey of self-discovery, one that defies convention and brings into question the most basic aspect of his being. It begins as a bet made between student waiters over who makes more tips, males or females. To determine this, they agree to a rather unorthodox experiment. Though feigning reluctance, Andy accepts the challenge of taking on the role of female waitress as part of the bet.

The original purpose is forgotten as Andy finds that his female persona is more than an act, causing him to question his gender identity. His behavior while Amanda—the name he has given his female persona—does not escape the notice of his friends. Along with Andy, they conclude that their experiment is having unintended consequences. Rather than stopping, Andy uses the opportunity to determine who he really is and where he belongs on the gender continuum. In the process he discovers that there is a vast difference between sex and gender. This already bewildering situation becomes even more complicated when a male college student becomes smitten with Amanda.
(https://stephaniecastle.ca/tips/)

PUBLICATION EXPECTED IN 2021
A Different Kind of Courage
Newly Chronicles: Volume II
H. W. Coyle

How does a person go about rebuilding a life that they willingly tried to throw away? For Andrew Newly, this journey begins by realizing it will take a different kind of courage. His efforts begin by returning to where he and a group of friends bought into a crazy bet that changed his life forever. Together with those friends, he struggles to gather up the frayed threads of his life and begin the daunting task of building a new one for himself, this time as a girl named Amanda. Amanda finds that she must not only find a way of dealing with problems that are as confusing to her as they are complex, she must also come to terms with a past that seems to have no place in her new life. This difficult journey is complicated by Amanda's friendship with Tina Anderson, the daughter of an entrepreneur who has accumulated a fair number of enemies who prove to be as much of a threat to Amanda as they are to the Andersons, causing her to draw upon a past that she is trying to put behind her.

(https://stephaniecastle.ca/a-different-kind-of-courage/)

PUBLICATION EXPECTED IN 2021
Inconvenient Truths
Newly Chronicles: Volume III
H.W. Coyle

Living on the edge with nothing but a safety net woven from lies to keep you from tumbling headlong into disaster and disgrace is as dangerous as it is demanding. For Amanda Newly, it is an inconvenient fact of life, one she must deal with every day.

Amanda is a unique college student, bright and intelligent. To the casual observer, Amanda presents the very image of a young woman on the verge of making all her dreams come true. The only thing holding Amanda back from achieving this elusive goal is a past that is totally out of sync with her image as a vibrant young coed, for the girl everyone knows as Amanda started life as Andrew Justin Newly.

In many ways Amanda is still very male, an inconvenient truth she must hide behind a veil of lies as she struggles to reconcile her past with her future. One aspect of Amanda's past that threatens to destroy her chances is not of her own making. Tina Anderson, the daughter of a wealthy entrepreneur and one of Amanda's dearest friends lives under a constant threat of kidnapping, a danger that Amanda once foiled, leaving her vulnerable to retribution from those seeking to bring harm to the Andersons.

Amanda's journey toward a new beginning is one that is as difficult as it is contentious. For she must step outside the accepted norms, which define who and what we are, in order to discover not only what is right for her, but to build a new life for herself.
(https://stephaniecastle.ca/inconvenient-truths/)

Coming in 2021/2022 from
Castle Carrington Publishing
You have a story. Let us help you tell it
https://transgenderpublishing.ca/

PUBLICATION EXPECTED IN 2021
Pushing the Boundaries!
How to Get More Out of Life
Peter Jennings

Pushing The Boundaries! How To Get More Out Of Make Life features profiles of 32 people from around the world (many of whom are well-known and featuring many Canadians) who reveal how they triumph in life. We're talking people who have overcome uneasiness about taking risks, like daredevil Nik Wallenda; doctor-of-change, Patch Adams; intersex supermodel, Hanne Gaby Odielle; international clothing designer, Tommy Hilfiger. Also included are Canadians like Marina Nemat, who defied certain execution in her teens at Evin prison in Tehran; McDonald's of Canada Chair, George Cohon, who persevered through 14 years to break into the Russian market; Rick Hansen, who pushed himself around the world in a wheelchair to raise awareness of people with disabilities; Katie Taylor who's broken the glass ceiling by becoming the first female Chair of a major Canadian Bank; Donald Ziraldo, who put Inniskillin Winery on the map by making Icewine into an immensely popular beverage worldwide; etc. As Jack Canfield, renowned co-author of the *Chicken Soup For The Soul*® series says in the book's Foreword, "Having the conviction to reach beyond your fears and take chances means you're ready to achieve lasting success."
(https://castlecarringtonpublishing.ca/pushing-the-boundaries/)

PUBLICATION EXPECTED IN 2021
Being Happy Matters
Peter Jennings

Being Happy Matters is a re-launch of a previously published book *Why Being Happy Matters*. The updated Introduction references COVID-19 and how happiness can be an antidote to the stress and anxiety people are experiencing right now. The original volume presents interviews with people in Canada, the US, Asia, Europe and Australia, each of whom reveal what happiness means to them and why it matters. Readers will meet international PhDs who are actively studying the science of positive psychology (i.e., happiness). This book features Peter Jennings in conversation with 37 intriguing individuals, including John Robbins, heir of the Baskin Robbins empire (who tells Peter about turning down his inheritance and then losing his life's savings in the Bernie Madoff scandal, but still exhibiting a positive outlook of happy perseverance to life's reversals); Roko Belic, California-based Oscar-nominated director of the award-winning film "Happy"; Dr. Christine Carter, sociologist and positive psychology specialist at Berkeley University ; Rolling Stones keyboardist Chuck Leavell (who shared with Peter the joy he gets from working with his buddy former President Jimmy Carter on key environmental issues); Major League Baseball legend Shawn Green; celebrated super-model & businesswoman Monika Schnarre; Time magazine humour columnist Joel Stein; 84 year old Playboy cartoonist Doug Sneyd; Leo Bormans from Belgium, author of the respected "World Book of Happiness"(who explains what lies behind his discussions with global experts); and much more.
(https://castlecarringtonpublishing.ca/being-happy-matters/)

Coming in 2021/22 from
Perceptions Press
Publishing innovative, avant-garde (and occasionally
provocative) transgender fiction and non-fiction
https://perceptionspress.ca/

PUBLICATION EXPECTED IN 2021
Parably Not
Will2Love Series Book 3
Paul Van Der Spiegel

Parably Not is Book 3 of the *Will2Love Series.*

William Blake wrote in the preface to *Jerusalem The Emanation of the Giant Albion* of his desire to "speak to future generations by a Sublime Allegory." One could also argue that the miracles and the parables of Christ are metaphors, and one of the errors of the religion that bears their name is trampling sublime allegory beneath the heel of process and doctrine.

If *Trans Deus* is Mark, if *7 Minutes* is Matthew, then *Parably Not* is Lucy with the dynamic of "Q Source" thrown in for good measure. "Q" is not a ridiculous conspiracy theory cooked up to delude and obfuscate a population. "Q" is the theory proposed by biblical scholars to account for the shared content in Matthew and Luke, the oral "sayings of Jesus" tradition that is absent in Mark's account. We can only speculate on who Quelle was, but it wouldn't surprise me if they were a woman, or a group of women—a female gospel airbrushed from history by the patriarchy that followed. As someone who passionately believes in inclusion and diversity, it was not too much of a leap to make my Q Source a queer source.

Having written two "text only" books, I wanted to emulate the Prophet of Hercules Road and illuminate these recontextualised parables, continuing the process I had pioneered as a child, cutting up my mum's copies of *Woman's Own* and pasting the chosen pages into my scrapbook.

"We were worried about you for a while," my dad told me as a teenager, as he recollected my enthusiasm for *Woman's Weekly*, sparkly tights, and walking about in my mum's heels carrying her handbag. I said nothing.

"Poetry fetter'd, fetters the human race," Blake wrote. He's right. But there are plenty of other things that fetter the human race, too.

Our job as sub-creators is to unfetter, to explore, to challenge, to remake. I offer you *Parably Not*, as it is intended: scrapbook literature, unfinished, scruffy, feral, confused, uncertain; ready to be woven into new allegory.

(https://perceptionspress.ca/parably-not/)

PUBLICATION EXPECTED IN 2021
Eman8
Will2Love Series Book 4
Paul Van Der Spiegel
Eman8 is Book 4 of the *Will2Love Series*.
(https://perceptionspress.ca/eman8/)

Coming in 2021/22 from
All Genders Press
Publishing LGBTQ+ fiction and non-fiction
https://perceptionspress.ca/

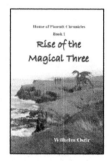

PUBLICATION EXPECTED IN 2021
Rise of the Magical Three
House of Phoenix Chronicles Book 1
Wilhelm Ostir
Raised by a mysterious grandmother and believing their parents to be dead, Roslynn and her older identical twin brothers, Oliver and Ethan, had only read of magical beings and creatures. But, transitioning into young adulthood, the three embark on an incredible journey as they are introduced to the riddles of their family's past that will forever change who they are and are yet to become. As the three siblings discover the ways of the magical arts, they quickly learn that they are not alone in their quest. Finding help when and where they least expect, the three develop friendships, confront the darkness, work together to save their family from an ancient curse, and learn of a mysterious and ancient bloodline that will forever shape the fabric of time and love. Their fight becomes more significant than even they had anticipated and forces them to make decisions about whether they can effectively save the world, the multiple realms, and magic as they know it. Learning that magic is driven by passion, knowledge, bloodline, and time, will they be the ones to save time, or will they become mere echoes of time? (https://allgenderspress.ca/echoes-of-time/)

The **House of Phoenix Chronicles** *is planned as a series of books filled with wizards, witches, fairies, elves, dwarfs, centaurs, mermaids, and dragons in the fight of their lives to protect their ways of life, their families, and the earth. The Phoenix siblings, Rosalynn and her older identical twin brothers, Oliver and Ethan, embark on a remarkable journey of friendship, romance,* *hatred, and mystery as truths are revealed, challenges faced, and battles with ancient darkness fought. Bending magic to their will, Roslynn, Ethan and Oliver, step in and out of time, breaking the rules at every stage of their remarkable journey. Along their way, they meet friends from the past, present, and future, and discover an ancient secret that could forever change the fabric of history, including our understanding of Medieval times and the Knights of the Round Table: a curse sent by darkness to unravel time as it is known. One minute, magic was at its height, the center of life and the community. In the next, cities and villages lay in ruins, a mere echo of a time that was. Can the three siblings channel their family's magic, one of the most powerful magical bloodlines ever to live, for good? Or will their efforts backfire, leading to the destruction of all magical beings? Will they be able to break the curse that affects their family? Can they save their bloodline and the ways of magic? Will they help bring magic back to earth, or will they become the continuation of the curse?*